What people are
Healing Your Marriage When Trust Is

This is a supernatural story of God's redemption and restoration. A man chose humility, his wife believed God for the impossible, and it happened. *Healing Your Marriage When Trust Is Broken* will give you hope for your marriage and strengthen your faith in a God who can turn our mistakes into miracles.

STEVEN FURTICK
lead pastor of Elevation Church
author of *Sun Stand Still*

What you are about to read is an all-too-real story of a couple in ministry whose marriage and vocation are suddenly rocked and halted by the consequences of infidelity. Chillingly honest but remarkably encouraging, Cindy's journey is one that breaks through the barriers of shock, pain, and betrayal to forgiveness, strength, and restoration. I look forward to sharing this book with so many I know who are dealing with the unfortunate devastation of a marital affair.

PETE WILSON
pastor of Cross Point Church
author of *Plan B*

One of the greatest gifts we can give to each other is the gift of knowing that we are not alone. Through Cindy's transparency and openness, she willingly gives this gift to all her readers. Need encouragement? Need hope? Need to know you aren't alone? Then please read *Healing Your Marriage When Trust Is Broken*.

JUD WILHITE
senior pastor of Central Christian Church
author of *Throw It Down*
founder of *leadingandlovingit.com*

Chris and Cindy's story is an inspirational and captivating account of humility, forgiveness, and redemption. Through the pain of betrayal, their story reflects the love of God that penetrates darkness to illuminate a new hope for marriages in crisis.

CHRIS HODGES
senior pastor of Church of the Highlands

With elegance, vulnerability, and grit, Cindy Beall shares what is every married woman's greatest nightmare. A powerful story of hope, an honest journey of struggle, an inspiring passage of renewal...the chronicle of Cindy's major life interruption speaks to the deepest place in my heart. This book is more than just a book on marital infidelity. It is a picture of the restorative love of Jesus, able to supersede any difficulty and compelling enough to make ugly things become beautiful. I love Chris and Cindy Beall's story. It is the story of Jesus.

LISA WHITTLE
speaker and author of {w}hole

This is a refreshing story of forgiveness, grace, and a pure desire to defeat the odds by saving a marriage that was on the verge of ending. If you are walking down the path of divorce, this book will inspire you not to give up, but to give your marriage to God and watch Him work a miracle.

DINO RIZZO
lead pastor of Healing Place Church

Cindy Beall's message of grace is simple but profound: Jesus is your hope for a successful marriage. No matter where you find yourself, her story will challenge and inspire you to let God heal the past and build a better future.

JUDAH SMITH
lead pastor of The City Church, Seattle, Washington

I was randomly placed with the Bealls a few years back for an evening that turned out to be a ministry-shifting moment in my life. I was captivated that evening as the authenticity flowed from Cindy's story on hurt, hope, and the resurrection of an undying love. This book took me back to that night. Cindy's words will rip the veil off any fear and doubt that God can heal you in spite of your own best effort.

CARLOS WHITTAKER
worship leader

If you are a skeptic who believes miracles no longer exist, or if you are in the thick of pain and think God has left, I ask you to read this book. What happened in Chris and Cindy's life and the healing that came to their marriage cannot be anything short of a miracle. Low odds, indescribable pain, and bleak circumstances were all God needed to do what He does best—the impossible. If you need hope that God still does the impossible, this is your book.

NATALIE WITCHER
author of The Devil in Your Garden

So honest…So real…So transparent…So timely. Being in leadership, I've seen the devastation of a husband and wife who didn't know how to put the pieces back together again. Cindy does such an excellent job of using word pictures to describe her journey of healing and restoration. This book will help couples rebuild *trust* in a broken marriage.

SHEILA GERALD
pastor of Champions Centre, Tacoma, Washington

Healing Your Marriage When Trust Is Broken

CINDY BEALL

Foreword by CRAIG GROESCHEL

HARVEST HOUSE PUBLISHERS

EUGENE, OREGON

Cover by Koechel Peterson & Associates, Inc., Minneapolis, Minnesota

Cover photo © iStockphoto / davidp

Backcover photo © Amanda Hyden

This book contains stories in which the author has changed people's names and some details of their situations in order to preserve their privacy.

HEALING YOUR MARRIAGE WHEN TRUST IS BROKEN
Copyright © 2011 by Cindy Beall
Published by Harvest House Publishers
Eugene, Oregon 97402
www.harvesthousepublishers.com

Library of Congress Cataloging-in-Publication Data
Beall, Cindy, 1970-
Healing your marriage when trust is broken / Cindy Beall; foreword by Craig Groeschel.
    p. cm.
    ISBN 978-0-7369-4315-4 (pbk.)
    ISBN 978-0-7369-4316-1 (eBook)
    1. Marriage—Religious aspects—Christianity. 2. Sex addiction—Religious aspects—Christianity. 3. Adultery. 4. Pornography—Religious aspects—Christianity. 5. Trust—Religious aspects—Christianity. I. Title.
    BV835.B357 2011
    241'.667092—dc22
    [B]
                                                                    2010050358

Printed in the United States of America

12 13 14 15 16 17 18 19 / VP-NI / 10 9 8 7 6 5 4 3

In honor and in memory of my father,
Joe Ernest Moehring,
and my father-in-law,
Charles Joseph Beall

Contents

Foreword

by Pastor Craig Groeschel

WHEN CHRIS BEALL, MY NEW STAR WORSHIP LEADER, confessed to me that he'd been unfaithful to his wife, Cindy, I could have vomited on the spot.

Overwhelming emotions flooded my heart. Shock. Disappointment. Anger. Sadness.

Questions pelted my mind like hail smashing against a sidewalk during a storm. How did this happen? Why didn't I see it? What am I going to tell our church? What will Cindy do? Will their marriage survive this blow?

I'll never forget seeing the deep and seemingly unrecoverable hurt in Cindy's eyes when she discovered the devastating truth.

Behind the scenes, we did the only things we knew to do. We prayed a lot. We cried a lot. We read a lot of Scriptures.

We gathered the elders of the church to consider how to move forward. Our top goal was to minister to Chris and Cindy and help them decide what to do next. Chris' actions obviously disqualified him from his pastoral role.

With the weekend approaching, I knew that I'd have to make some sort of public statement. Unfortunately, church leaders often fail to navigate the rough waters of moral failure successfully. Churches are often mortally wounded following this type of public failure.

Without knowing quite what to do, I simply decided to tell the truth.

"Chris betrayed his wife and will no longer be serving in his role as our worship leader." Without going into detail, I compassionately explained that one of our brothers had fallen and that as a church, we'd do everything within our power to help his marriage heal.

We agreed to pray for the miracle of restoration for this family. I talked to our church about the Hebrew word that is translated as *restore*. The word *shuwb* literally means "to be made better than new." "With Christ's healing work," I declared by faith, "one day Chris and Cindy's marriage could be better than new."

The next Sunday, Chris and Cindy Beall walked into church and sat side by side as the wounded but loving church embraced them.

This was the beginning of the arduous uphill climb to put a broken marriage back together. Through Chris and Cindy's counseling, tears, hard work, perseverance, courage, accountability, and raw self-abandoned forgiveness, God has done what only He can do. He has made the Beall family better than new.

Nine years later, Chris is serving on our staff again—as the pastor of our largest campus. Cindy writes and speaks to help marriages all over the world.

This book is the most honest journey of healing I've ever read. Cindy bears all without pulling any punches. Her transparency will win you. Her courage will inspire you. Her story will change you.

If you've faced betrayal and wonder if healing is possible, this book is God's gift to you.

Craig Groeschel
pastor of LifeChurch.tv

When the Walls Come Tumbling Down

You never forget the day that changes your life forever. The day that turns your heart and your family upside down. But when that day begins, you don't realize it's anything out of the ordinary.

It was February 19, 2002, and my husband of nine years, Chris, and I were just getting settled into our new home in Edmond, Oklahoma. He had come out six weeks earlier on his own to begin his ministry with LifeChurch.tv as the worship pastor of the Edmond Campus. I had stayed behind in Memphis to wrap up the sale of our home there. But now we and our almost three-year-old son, Noah, were happily back together under one roof.

On this morning, while Chris was at the church, I was doing the usual stuff that nesters do. I unpacked boxes, fought with bubble wrap, and put away our belongings in the kitchen, the bathrooms, and the rest of the house. I was enjoying the process and thought how good it was to prepare our new home for this new life we had prayed about so fervently.

And then Chris came home unexpectedly at 9:30.

I was about to ask why he was back from work so soon, but the worried expression on his face stopped me from saying anything. He asked if we could talk. The request sounded so formal and distant that my heart raced as I quickly and silently got Noah settled in front of our TV with a Blue's Clues video and inched my way along a narrow path around stacks of boxes and toward Chris. My mind was spinning in anticipation of what might come out of his mouth.

Had one of our parents died or been in an accident? Had the church changed their mind about adding Chris to the staff?

Chris motioned me to the newly purchased sofa, and we sat down together. I tried to look into his handsome green eyes for reassurance. But those amazing, clear eyes that had captivated me the day we met years before were now downcast. I waited for him to reassure me that all was well in this new life. But instead of words of comfort, the man I had prayed for as a young woman, long before I knew him, was about to share news that would alter the course of our lives in unimaginable ways.

The Prayers of a Young Woman

I first prayed for my future husband while I was serving as a summer missionary on a Native American reservation in Wyoming. Although this ministry experience would become one of the best challenges and inspirations in my life and faith journey, the day I had to say goodbye to my mom at the Austin, Texas, airport was an unhappy one. The cute denim jumper with the cheery sailor collar I wore did little to dress up my sadness at having to leave her and my home to be 1200 miles away for 11 weeks. It felt like a world and a lifetime apart.

The first couple of weeks proved to be difficult. My tear-stained cheeks initially put a damper on the adventure. But eventually I understood that I needed this time to grow up and learn to rely on God.

And I did.

I learned a lot about the woman I would become. I not only learned to lean on God but also discovered that I had a voice and something to say and something worth sharing. I learned that not all things make sense when you follow Christ. And I realized it's okay to not have an answer for everything. In fact, it's actually more authentic and appealing when you don't.

In the midst of my time of learning about God, about others, and most definitely about myself, I had a longing in my heart for true love. The kind of love that would lead me to say to someone special, "I want to spend the rest of my life with you." And I wasn't the type of girl who had to have a boyfriend on her arm at all times. For one thing, I was taller than most guys my age. This is hardly an asset for a young girl's dating potential. I also possessed an independent spirit, and I liked the freedom I was experiencing during this stage of life.

Still, this longing for true love grew. I would be turning 21 soon, and although there isn't a guideline or time frame that says young women should fall in love by this age, I definitely wouldn't have pushed the opportunity away. *If* it was the right guy, you understand. *My* right guy.

One particular July night during that summer mission, I stared out at the beautiful mountains bathed in sunset's glow and began praying for others and for my future husband. At that moment, the idea popped into my head—thank You, Holy Spirit—that maybe I should pray for my husband's salvation. So I did.

I prayed that my future husband would have the character, personality, talents, passions, and even the looks that matched up with the list I made about the man of my dreams. I didn't think I was asking for much. Just the moon, the stars, and everything in between. Why not, right?

I first saw Chris Beall at a barn dance in November 1991. We couldn't take our eyes off each other. He wasn't the best dresser, nor did he have a model-perfect smile, but he held my gaze with those intoxicating green eyes. I was smitten almost immediately.

Almost.

It would be a few more months before anything actually began between us. He started frequenting the Baptist Student Union on our campus for our Wednesday lunches. Within a few weeks, at one of those lunches, he asked me for a dinner date the following Monday. I didn't have to agonize with anticipation for five days. Instead, he came to my church on Sunday and invited me out to lunch with a group of friends. There was so much excitement and "I can't believe this is really happening" in the air that by Sunday evening, we found ourselves sitting on the balcony of my apartment eating mint chocolate chip ice cream and talking about life, family, and mostly about Jesus. And I found out something special about Chris that evening: He'd been a Christ follower for less than a year, and the date that he gave his life to Christ was July 7, 1991—the summer that the Holy Spirit led me to pray for my future husband's salvation.

Big sigh.

I knew with every part of my being that Chris Beall was the one for me. I knew it beyond a shadow of a doubt. I knew it in my knower and felt it in my feeler. But what I didn't know was that the very next day he made a down payment on my wedding ring.

Ten months later, on January 9, 1993, we became husband and wife.

We were so madly in love with Jesus and each other that we were certain we'd conquer it all. We never would have guessed that the road we'd travel together over the course of our marriage would be anything but bliss.

Love was completely blind in our case. It's a good thing, because little did I know that around year nine, we'd get our sight back.

Confession

I sat down next to Chris on our new couch, and as he began speaking, my throat went dry and my eyes stung with hot tears. Even though shock was making it hard for my mind to make sense of the words and phrases and sentences, my heart and soul took it all in with great sorrow. Chris wasn't communicating the news that someone we loved was hurt. He was confessing that he, the person I loved most in the world, had hurt and betrayed me in the deepest way.

Chris had been unfaithful.

I was now trembling head to foot as my mind continued to spin with disbelief. I felt nauseous as the confession continued. He had been unfaithful with more than one woman. In fact, he had been with many women in many different places over the course of the past two and a half years.

While I listened, the very real physical pain of a heart breaking took me by surprise. And as I struggled to keep breathing, Chris forced himself to speak the last part of his confession through trembling lips: One of the women was pregnant, and he was pretty sure the baby was his child.

He kept his eyes on me. He didn't look away for a minute, even when my face clearly changed. His eyes were tender, and I could tell he was devastated by watching me. He didn't reach out for me right away. He seemed to be in shock that he was actually confessing. Then, as the reality set in of what his news was doing to my heart, he began to cry.

Many angry thoughts could have rushed through my mind at that point, but the unfathomable absurdity of this surreal, frozen moment in time triggered one thought over and over, "You have got to be kidding me!"

He was definitely not kidding.

He sat there just waiting for me to respond. I was stunned and couldn't make sense of what had just happened. I sifted through emotions and terms for emotions. It was none of them specifically and all of them collectively. Bewildered. Stunned. Shocked. Overwhelmed. Befuddled. Floored. Jolted. Nauseated. Sickened. Disturbed. Crushed. Dismayed. Paralyzed.

Ticked off. And that's putting it nicely.

The truth is that I still can't tell you to this day how I felt in those first few moments. What I can tell you is that I was keenly aware that my world as I knew it was forever changed. I woke up that morning a relatively comfortable housewife and stay-at-home mom, and within a couple of hours I became a seriously damaged woman with a marriage on the brink of destruction.

We had both made vows to forsake all others for the rest of our lives. I had kept my vow. He had not. Even when the distance between us grew, I kept mine. He had not. Even when other men showed interest in me, I kept mine. He had not. Even when days came where I didn't even want to spend time with him, I kept mine. He had not.

When the Walls Fall Down

I was deeply wounded by the truth about the lies that poured from my loved one that morning. I ached not only for me but also for the new church that had hired and embraced Chris. For our son. For our families. For our friends. As the walls of the life we had built came tumbling down, hard realization after hard realization, I felt them crush the foundations of our shared life and the dreams of this new chapter we were entering.

Can you relate to that kind of letdown? Destruction? Betrayal? When the walls have fallen down with such force that you could not breathe beneath the pressure of the debris or see beyond the dust of the rubble?

My spirit was broken that morning. My heart was shattered. Thoughts of moving forward in life or taking positive action would have sounded absurd had anyone been there to suggest them. I could barely conceive of moving my body from that place on the couch. In fact, the only reason I was able to stand up and move was that the impulse to step away from Chris was so strong. I wanted to be as removed from him physically as I felt from him emotionally in that moment. I had never, ever felt so alone.

If you are feeling alone, know that I am here to journey with you, and so is God. He already desires to make you whole, even as the pieces of your known existence seem to be scattered to every corner of the universe. If the walls have tumbled and you cannot recognize truth from lies in the remains, know that God's grace and power to transform your life are right there in the midst of the debris.

Hold on to your belief in redemption.

I kept mine. Please keep yours as we walk together toward healing.

Your Healing Journey

1. Has your spouse ever caught you off guard with a heartbreaking confession? If so, what was your initial response?

2. Have you ever had to make a confession that you knew would break your loved one's heart? What finally helped you break your cycle of lies?

3. Have you ever received news that altered your life in a dramatic way? What was it, and how did you handle it? If you are able, take yourself back there mentally and allow God to bring healing as you grieve what you lost and as you journey through this book.

4. What happens when we bottle up our emotions and choose not to deal with them? Do you know people who do this? Has this been you? How can you become more able to share or express your emotions?

5. Discuss ways you can remain committed to your marriage even when you don't feel like it or when circumstances have caused a lack of connection between you and your spouse.

2

The Storm
of Questions

DID YOU DISCOVER YOUR SPOUSE'S LIE, unfaithfulness, or secret sin on your own, or did he or she share it with you? I believe that no matter how one spouse uncovers a difficult truth about the other's behavior, thoughts, or actions, there is an initial shock that freezes the flow of time while allowing a hundred thoughts to spin and collide. I always thought the belief that one's life flashes before his or her eyes right before death was exaggerated—that is, until I sat on that couch and stared into my husband's distraught face while a tornado of thoughts, worries, memories, and questions swirled across my mind.

At first my questions were a stuttered series of single words: What? When? Where? And of course the all-time favorite question asked by thousands when thrown into unwanted circumstances: Why?

But eventually the storm of more fleshed-out questions began. Why in the world would you choose to do this? Why did you need other women?

Wasn't I enough? Why so many? Were you in love with any of them? Where did it happen? When did it happen?

What did you do with them? What did they do to you?

How many times? Did it happen in our home? Did it happen in our bed?

Do I mean anything to you? Was it all a farce?

Did our ministry mean anything? How did you lead others to Jesus while you were living this life on the side?

Chris knew those questions would be coming, and as I asked, he simply sat there and cried.

After we regained some composure, he assured me that it wasn't my fault. He told me that he loved me and found me attractive. He told me I was a great wife. He said he loved being married to me. He told me he never loved any of the women. He told me that his relationship with Jesus was real and that he did love the teenagers to whom we had ministered.

Then I asked him the only coherent thought I could conjure up at the moment: "Why on earth would you risk what we have to be with someone else?"

He replied, "Because I'm addicted to pornography."

The Questions Keep Coming

Being completely caught off guard with his response, I sat there in stunned silence. I let my mind go wild with wonder. Within a few minutes I began to consider how I would exist as a single mom raising my son. I figured that I would need to teach elementary school again for a living. Getting a position anywhere would be difficult because I'd been out of the classroom for more than four years. My heart sank even more at the thought of Noah in daycare. It was a privilege for me to stay home and raise him. I saw myself losing that privilege.

I wondered how Chris would make a living to support himself, us, and his new child with another woman. Our current financial situation barely got us by every month. How would it get all of us by in three different households? My livelihood would be affected. I would need his financial support to make it through because at 31, I surely didn't want to live off my mother. Asking her to help me get on my feet was going to be hard enough.

This new burden was heavier than any I'd ever experienced. And the only reason I now carried this burden was that my husband could carry it no more. That was the cold, hard reality about my situation. It was a very selfish move on his behalf, I thought. What made Chris think he could just dump all his junk on me, lightening his load while I suffocated under the weight of his confession?

I decided to take a shower because I felt dirty. As the water began to hit my body, all I could do was cry. Actually, crying is not quite an accurate description. I think weeping and all-out sobbing would be better. I was convulsing so much in my pain that an onlooker might have thought I was having a seizure. I was obviously loud, because Chris came in and made an attempt to comfort me. I immediately turned away from him. After all, his actions were the source of my pain. Then, a moment later, I was wishing his arms were around me—to comfort me, to protect me from this pain. It was very confusing to love and hate my husband at the same time.

I tried to control my tears around Noah, but that was just too difficult to accomplish. In his innocent little way, he tried to comfort me. I remember him asking, "Why you so sad, Mommy?"

Should a child who is a week away from his third birthday have to comfort his devastated mother? Should his world be wrecked because his daddy made horrible choices? It wasn't fair. Nothing about this situation was fair. And yet it was here. It filled our living room, our house, the space between Chris and me on the couch, the space where a full heart had been inside of me. The thoughts and questions that filled my mind were not about a distant situation; they were about my life.

A Bunch of Worst Days

I thought that February 19, 2002, was the worst day of my life. I would soon find that it was just the first in a series of days that would take me to places I'd never imagined. I'd always considered myself a hopeful person, but I remember begging God to take my life. I even went so far as to explain to God how He could orchestrate it when Noah wasn't in the car. All it would take was one little swerve in my overpriced SUV, and the pain would end. I just wanted to die. Surely living in His presence would be far better than living this life on earth.

I knew the psalm that said joy would come in the morning, but that was not my reality. Not that God's Word wasn't and isn't true, but sorrow became an ever-present companion as I awoke each morning to begin the day with my son. The odd thing was that as each day progressed, I felt better. By the evenings, I might even laugh a little or watch some mindless sitcom. Staying up late at night brought me more comfort. I guess I hoped the morning would not come. When it did, my first waking thought was of the state of my marriage. As my eyelids opened and my mind checked in to my surroundings, my new reality set in and I was slammed against a wall. Every single morning. It was almost as if I was reliving Chris' confession to me on a daily basis.

I am not a proponent of abortion, but I must confess that it sounded like a very convenient option at the time. Consumed by my own grief, I wasn't even thinking about the other woman's life or circumstances. I could not believe this was unfolding before me. Why in the world didn't my husband protect himself—protect us? How on earth was I going to explain to my son that he has a brother but I'm not his brother's mom? It was far too overwhelming for my mind to handle. I simply could not believe the choices my husband had made. They were killing me. And they had to have been breaking Jesus' heart.

I still could not wrap my mind around the fact that an addiction to pornography led him to do such awful things. I thought he had just looked at a few naked girls from time to time on the Internet. I thought he wasn't struggling with this very much anymore. I thought we were communicating fairly well on this subject. I thought that's why he met with his accountability group on Fridays.

Apparently, I thought wrong.

When Chris explained his journey with porn, he shared that it began before he ever left his childhood home. He found a *Playboy* magazine in his house when he was eight. Not to mention the years of thumbing through *National Geographic* magazines, hoping to see a naked indigenous woman. What? You know you did it too.

Then there was an older guy from the neighborhood who worked at a convenience store in town. This guy would bring home the old issues of certain magazines that weren't read for the articles. The guy gave them to Chris and his friends, and they sat in a nearby tree house and looked at them. Day after day, they'd look.

As Chris grew older, pornography became much more easily accessible. He was now old enough to feed his own addiction and no longer needed to rely on a convenience-store clerk.

Some years later, as online porn sites emerged, all it took was the click of a mouse. And if you were really savvy, you could view pornography without paying a dime. A naked girl here and there. A couple engaging in intercourse. But soon those images no longer appealed to my husband. He needed something more. His sickness grew and grew and gave birth to more unhealthy desires. Eventually, after years of progression, this sin completely entangled him, and he acted out.

I now know it was just a matter of time. Sin never gets smaller. It always grows.

I felt smothered with hopelessness when I realized what a deep-seated sin this was in Chris' life. I still didn't know if I would stay in this very broken marriage or walk away. Yet at the same time, I remember having a single thought that brought some relief: "So it wasn't my fault after all."

Community Response

We had a truckload of devastation to wade through, and so did our church. Within the hour of Chris' confession, our pastor, Craig Groeschel, came over with Jerry, another pastor. The looks on their faces were pitiful. I know they wanted to say something that would make things better, but they just couldn't. So Craig hugged me as if there were no tomorrow. I mean, his embrace was so long that I thought he was trying to hug the pain out of me. It was an honorable and under-standable gesture, but it couldn't do the trick.

I imagine Craig felt helpless, not only because of what this would mean for LifeChurch.tv but also because he'd only known me six months, and just a couple of weeks of that time was spent living in the same town. So to say that Craig and I were close friends at the time would not be accurate. That would soon change.

If you've been around the Christian church for any length of time (regardless of the denomination), you have more than likely heard your share of stories about fallen pastors. My husband had been in full-time vocational ministry for six years. Our story was now one of those sad cases.

That Tuesday morning was one of the longest periods of time in my life. I wasn't sure where to go next, and neither was Craig. But within a couple of days, he made a decision that would ultimately turn out to be the best decision ever. However, getting to the end result would mean that Chris and I would have to be humbled like never before.

Shedding Light on Sin

I didn't even bother to put on makeup that week. People kept com-ing over to our house, mainly staff members and a few in leadership roles, and when I saw the sad, pathetic look in their eyes, I knew they were reflecting my own sad, pathetic face.

Two days after Chris' confession, Jerry and Lanita came over to dis-cuss the next steps for the church. LifeChurch.tv couldn't just hire a guy to lead worship and then six weeks later say, "Chris decided to take a break from ministry." What a farce—though I believe many churches would have done just that, which makes me thankful for our pastor's wisdom and integrity.

Craig is one of the most honorable men I know. He loves truth and righteousness so much that the staff at LifeChurch.tv sometimes says the environment there feels like spiritual sandpaper. If you are living in sin and working at LifeChurch.tv, chances are you will eventually either confess your sin or just quit. The high standard is hard to keep if you are continually gratifying your flesh.

Jerry and Lanita sat down with us and told us that Craig wanted to face our situation head-on with the church. They explained that Craig thought he should share our story with our entire campus. But he would not do it without our approval—a signed and notarized affidavit stating that we agreed with this approach.

My husband immediately said yes. Looking back now I can see just how hungry he was to get free from a life that he hated living. But at the time, I was downright petrified. I didn't know how our people would respond, and quite frankly, I wasn't interested in finding out. I wanted to walk out the door and never look back.

But I didn't because of the mortgage documents I'd signed just two weeks prior. I agreed to sign the affidavit, and three days later, Craig shared our story with our entire campus. I supported him sharing our story 100 percent. I'm not saying I wasn't scared half to death, because I absolutely was. Good grief, can you just imagine how you'd feel knowing that your entire life was going to be preached about to a few thousand people? That they'd hear what your husband did while ministering as a pastor? That they'd learn that he wasn't who he said he was? That maybe they'd think you weren't good enough to keep your man satisfied? Exactly.

Yep. I was scared. And frankly, I wasn't even completely sure I was going to stay married to him. So when I heard the tape of Craig's message that day, including the part when he told the congregation that I had chosen to stay with Chris, I was a little ticked off. I hadn't left my home and husband yet, but that didn't mean I had decided to stay.

Do I stay or not? That was the million-dollar question. And I needed a million-dollar answer. Pronto.

When the Questions Hinder Healing

Sometime during the first year after Chris' confession, I finally made a decision. Chris and I were discussing the past, and I don't remember exactly what I asked him, but it had something to do with an encounter he had with a woman. He very gently took my hand and said, "Babe, I'll answer any question you ask for the rest of my life. But will my answer make you feel any better?"

I looked into his eyes and knew he was right. The answer wouldn't make me feel better. The only thing it would do is tell me the date and time that he made a fool of me. I know that when I ask questions, it comes from a place of fear in me. My heart starts beating faster, and I literally don't have the physical or mental strength to stop moving forward in my quest for answers. So I stopped asking questions.

And maybe you should too. Some details—what your spouse did with whom or where they did it or how often it happened—aren't going to make your heart feel any better or your mind any clearer. I understand asking some questions in the beginning because you are just simply trying to grasp the entire situation. But after a while, it's just time to let it go and move on.

It's easy for me to just say, "Let it go," isn't it? But don't forget, I've been down the road you are now on. Heck, I took up residence on it for a while and had my own little piece of real estate on that street. I know how hard it is to let it go and stop asking questions. So here's what I did to walk myself through that.

When my curiosity got the best of me and I wanted to ask Chris something, I first asked myself two questions: Why do I need to know this? And will this help me heal? More times than not, asking the question would only hurt me more, which would not bring healing. Other times, the point of my question was just to find out when I'd been fooled, thus fueling a pride issue I was battling.

Ultimately, we must stop asking questions of our spouses because we trust our heavenly Father to make all things new again. Regardless of whether your marriage has survived, you must free yourself from the false need to gain more information because it will not help your journey to freedom.

Your Healing Journey

1. Can you identify with the emotions Cindy felt? What parts of her story strike a chord in your heart and soul? Even if it is painful, try to spend time with those emotions. Ask God for continued healing even if these emotions are tied to an event from long ago.

2. Have you had a painful experience that a lot of people knew about? How did that make you feel? Who can you talk to who is godly and wise?

3. If you've had "a bunch of worst days" just as Cindy did, how did you manage to get out of bed every day and go on with your life? What do you still need in order to do this if this heartbreak is fresh? Ask God for this need to be met.

4. When infidelity or another type of betrayal happens in a marriage, why do people struggle with the decision to stay or go?

5. Have you forgiven your spouse (or been forgiven) for something you never thought would be a part of your marriage?

6. Is it hard for you to believe that infidelity came from a pornography addiction? What addictions big or small plague you or your loved one? How can you work to change those behaviors before they get out of control?

A Story of Healing in Their Own Words

KEVIN AND NICOLE

ALL OF THE STORIES I WILL SHARE in the sections titled "A Story of Healing in Their Own Words" are similar and yet unique. Some of the stories began because the marriages were struggling and needs weren't being met. Some of the affairs began due to addictions to pornography. Some of those who were unfaithful were men; some were women. Or both. Some were in full-time ministry at a church; some worked outside the church. Some were parents; some were not.

Those who commit adultery come in all shapes, sizes, and races, and they are as different as can be. There is no mold that makes someone an adulterer. I do believe, however, that the marriages that survive adultery have some things in common. Both husband and wife are willing to forgive and receive forgiveness instead of living in shame. Both are willing to look inside their own lives and see how they could have contributed to making their marriage vulnerable. Both made choices even though they didn't always feel right.

Whether you have been on this road before or not, I hope you are encouraged by the hearts of these individuals who have chosen to get back up after such a testing and trying time. Adultery could have taken them out of the game and changed their futures for the worse forever, but they wouldn't have it.

Chris and I try to help as many couples as possible who have walked through infidelity in their marriage. We don't typically spend our off time with couples who just need some mentoring or just want to learn how to communicate better. That might sound harsh, rude, or even calloused, but the reality is that there are far too many couples who need our help to walk through the effects of their infidelity. And because we've been there and "have a file" on that subject, we try to help. I say "try" because not all couples are willing to do whatever it takes to make their marriages work. One spouse might be willing, but the other might just be giving lip service.

Still, over the years, we've come across some couples who have chosen to take the high road and hit their infidelity issues head-on. I'd like for you to hear from six couples. I wanted to take a little time to share some of their stories with you because we all love redemptive stories. (Somebody please say amen.)

These couples have opened up their hearts so that you might be encouraged by seeing how amazing our God is—even through the ugliness that accompanies adultery. You won't want to miss what they have to share. Here's our first story.

∽⊷◦

I hope I get to meet Kevin and Nicole face-to-face one day. Nicole and I have been e-mail friends for a couple of years now and have even talked on the phone. We tell each other about our husbands, and we think they might have been separated at birth. That's how similar they are.

Kevin and Nicole have lived their story publicly and are very open about their trials and healing. Kevin was addicted to pornography, and he eventually acted out multiple times with multiple people over a period of years. Sound familiar?

As you read about their journey, you will hear a richness. You will understand how deeply committed they are to Christ and to furthering His kingdom on earth even if they have to go through the valley of the shadow of death. I am seriously honored and humbled that God would use the pain Chris and I endured to minister to this precious couple. My Redeemer lives. So does yours.

∽⊷◦

CINDY: Nicole, what was your initial response when you found out about Kevin's infidelity?

NICOLE: I know it sounds crazy, but when Kevin was brought to me to confess, I laid my hands on him and prayed for him before I did anything else. It was all I knew to do. God had instantaneously communicated to me that I was looking into the face of someone who was very sick but who was finally free from hiding, someone who would have quite a journey in believing God's grace was enough for him.

But over the course of the next few hours, the pain, devastation, disbelief, shock, disorientation, raging fury, and deep, deep hurt flooded in. I felt as if a tidal wave had crashed into my life and I was bobbing along, just trying to keep my head above water.

CINDY: Kevin, did you ever think you'd do such a thing as commit adultery?

KEVIN: When I said "I do" on my wedding day, I never planned on ending up here. And the day I did "wake up," I had no idea how I had gotten to this place of total rebellion and self-indulgence. It was a fast, downward cycle fueled by pornography, lust, and low self-esteem. It was a sinful pit of hell.

CINDY: Nicole, what made you decide to stay?

NICOLE: One of the biggest things was that I had a spouse who was 100 percent committed to me and my children. He was so happy that his secret life was over and that he was so freely living under God's grace, he was able to love me and the kids in a new and deeper way. His lack of defensiveness and willingness to do whatever it took to heal himself and to facilitate my healing as well made all the difference.

CINDY: Kevin, how have you dealt with the pain you've seen in Nicole's eyes over the years?

KEVIN: I don't get defensive because I know that I created this journey. I know that I will have to fight for the rest of my life to win my wife's heart, trust, love, and soul back. I try to feel the pain instead of dismiss it.

CINDY: Nicole, how have you been able to forgive Kevin?

NICOLE: One day, I had a major breakthrough toward forgiveness, realizing that I would die if I continued to withhold it from him. With hope of freedom, I offered him forgiveness that day, but I am going through a continual process every day. Every time I choose not to dwell in the past, I am choosing to forgive. Every time I choose to hold my tongue when I just want to destroy him with it, I am choosing to forgive. Every time I choose to give my pain to God instead of punish Kevin with it, I am choosing to forgive. It is so hard. I don't think I'm there yet—wherever and whatever "there" is. But I'm pressing on.

CINDY: What is the state of trust in your marriage?

NICOLE: I can honestly say that Kevin made it very easy to trust him again. Once again, it goes back to his level of brokenness and his willingness to be healed and see me healed at all costs. He was so happy for his old life to be exposed and to finally understand what had gone so wrong, he willingly submitted himself to every measure of accountability put before him. I can say that this was probably the easiest part of the journey because of how he responded to the situation.

KEVIN: Right away I lived in strict accountability and called my accountability people daily. I gave my wife any information or help she asked for. I let her know where I was at all times. I stopped using the computer and started working on my relationship with God. I have stayed clean from porn and all things that were habits of my old life. I'm continuing to seek out other men for local accountability and to help me grow in my journey with God. I believe Nicole trusts me to never go back to where I've been. She knows I hated who I used to be.

CINDY: How is your marriage today?

NICOLE: In process. We're not where we want to be, but we're not where we were either. I have struggled with the slowness of this journey. I want to be healed and have the nice, neat little bow on top of our perfectly healed marriage. It's not there yet. But I'm finding joy in this journey. I'm learning how to live again. I want every stage of our story to be used by God to glorify what He has done and who He is. So many people say, "I can't believe how strong you are." And I always tell them, "You have no idea how weak I am. It is only because of Jesus that I am here and still alive." He is the hero of this story.

KEVIN: I feel as if we've reached a plateau. We're not sure what is next. We've been in survival mode for so long that we forget to just sit down, relax, and get to know each other again. With that said, I know we're not where we were, but we're far from being where I want us to be. We still have a long way to go. But I believe that God can once again breathe life into these dry bones and bring us back to life. I believe God is at work here and will complete what He started. I'm holding on to the promises from Isaiah 61:4: "They will rebuild the ancient ruins and restore the places long devastated; they will renew the ruined cities that have been devastated for generations."

3

The Quest for
Real Answers

I WISH I KNEW WHAT YOUR STRUGGLE WAS. Your path or your trial might be similar to mine or to Chris' or to the couples whose stories I highlight throughout this book. But you also have your own needs in this season of broken trust and healing. As you face something as devastating as unfaithfulness or disconnection in your relationship, you eventually realize that in order to heal, you have to deal with your personal decisions, your deep needs, and even your baggage. So while you focus on "the big incident" or the series of small betrayals, you will inevitably also be standing before a wall of your own needs.

As I mentioned earlier, I wanted answers—lots of them—but they were to the wrong questions. I know this because the answers didn't bring healing. They brought more pain. I was trying to reopen the wound over and over to try to make sense of it. But a wound that is not allowed to close will not heal. So what do you do?

You start looking for God's answers.

The one question I finally chose to focus on wasn't about what Chris had done in the past that had broken my heart. Rather, it was about what I would do in the future. Would I stay married to a man who had betrayed me and our holy union but who also appeared to have godly sorrow over his actions?

I felt as if everyone around me didn't want me to ask God the question about staying or going. They seemed to think that if I postponed the asking, maybe I would just stay in the marriage without any type of confirmation from God. Maybe they didn't want me to ask because they were afraid that somehow I would hear God incorrectly due to my damaged emotional state. Or maybe they were fearful that God would release me from my marriage, and then what do your loved ones, kids, friends, and church do with that? It gets complicated, doesn't it?

Healthy Leaving

Had I walked out the front door right after Chris' confession, it might have been hard to return. Ever. So I stayed several days to hear what Chris had to say, to shed tears, and to receive some initial godly counsel. Then I knew that it was time to step away for a bit. Seeing Chris and interacting with him each day renewed my pain, leaving me feeling trapped, surrounded, alone, and confused about my emotions. I needed a temporary escape so I could start processing the emotions and thoughts that were overloading my senses.

So I packed a few things for Noah and myself, and we went to see my mom in Texas for a week. She did a very good job of managing her own pain and frustration over my situation. She mostly listened and let me rush through my thought tangents and also rest in stretches of silence whenever I needed. I can't imagine being that coolheaded while watching my child get so deeply hurt, yet her response was exactly what I needed.

Mom made an appointment for me to see her pastor. I wasn't very excited about meeting with him because it sounded a bit like a chore, another futile exercise in humiliation and vulnerability. Hadn't I had enough of that in Oklahoma, the place I escaped from? And what in the world could this man, whom I didn't know, say to me that would help? My life was in shambles. My marriage seemed dead. My future was bleak at best. Did I really want to spread my sorrow and gloom throughout another state?

No.

But I went anyway. I was a 31-year-old wife and mom, but I was also my mother's baby girl. I decided to appease her and go to the appointment. I was too numb and tired to argue. The path of least resistance seems like a sensible option when you feel unable to make decisions.

On Tuesday, March 5, 2002, I had an appointment with Pastor Dan. I cried a lot in front of this stranger as I recounted the story. There was no condemnation in his words or actions. He was a true shepherd.

After spewing my story, which was starting to sound more unbelievable each time I told it, I awaited his pastoral response, which I was sure would sound very…well, pastoral. I'd been in ministry long enough to know that there are certain things that pastors say when bad things happen. I'd even said them as a pastor's wife. But I was praying that I wouldn't get such a response from him. I needed cold, hard advice that would tell me which path to take. Do I stay married to this man I pledged my life to that January day in 1993, or do I cut my losses, pack up my stuff, and hit the road? I needed an answer, and soon. My heart just couldn't take any more.

His response was very gracious and very pastoral. However, it was anything but a Sunday school answer and definitely not what I was expecting. He said, "I would respect you if you felt that you needed to remove yourself from your marriage. What you've endured is very hard. But you are not a fool to stay and be a part of the redemptive work in a man's life."

I can still hear him saying those words. I am not a fool to stay and be a part of the redemptive work in a man's life. Huh. Really? Because the last time I checked, the entire stinkin' world would say that I am. Once a cheater, always a cheater, right? Who in the world stays with a man who committed multiple acts of adultery and got a woman pregnant, all while sharing the love of Jesus as a pastor? Who does that?

Apparently I do.

His response to me was definitely unexpected, but I received it wholeheartedly. Two weeks had transpired since Chris' confession, and it was the first time in those 14 days when I felt any sense of peace or hope. Those two commodities had been absent from my heart, soul, body, and spirit since Chris dropped the bomb on me. And though I can't completely explain it to you, I knew Dan spoke on behalf of God. He was God's messenger disguised as a middle-aged Baptist minister.

Hope was in short supply at that point in my life. It's hard to define and make sense of, but you know when you have it, and you know when you don't. As I drove back to my mother's home, my childhood home, and pulled into the driveway, I was slightly encouraged and feeling just a little bit of hope.

Maybe our marriage could survive after all.

Maybe.

Longing for a Word from God

Dan's words were a beacon of light for me that day, but I still wasn't sure what my decision would be. I found myself asking God for more. I needed to hear from Him. I needed to know His plans and His answers for me and for my family's future. As hard as it was to deny my desire to bundle up my three-year-old and flee as far away from civilization as I could, I could not deny the commitment and surrender I made to the Lord in 1996 to serve in ministry. Despite Chris' actions, I knew the call to ministry wasn't just for him. It was for me too. Even though I never drew a paycheck, I was just as called to the church as he was. That was when I fully understood how the choices I made from this point on were not about reacting to Chris' confession, but about responding to God's leading—just as I would be asked to do in any other circumstances.

With this insight tucked in my heart and giving me a stronger sense of what I needed, I decided to go see my friend Ana-María in San Antonio and attend her church. I respected her pastor and just *knew* he'd be the one to tell me what God was leading me to do. Once I got to her house, she said that her pastor wouldn't be at church on this Sunday. I was disappointed; I had missed my chance for direction.

Nevertheless, once at church, I worshipped God through my tears. I honestly didn't care who saw me blubbering like an idiot. My story was known by the entire city of Edmond, Oklahoma, (or so I felt) and a few people in Georgetown, Texas. I could handle a few gray-haired women staring at me in San Antonio.

I listened intently to the message given by the guest speaker. I was afraid that I'd miss what God would say to me, and I was desperate because the next morning I was driving back to Oklahoma. I didn't want to go back to my husband without something to hold on to, something that would sustain me long enough to keep me from running for the hills.

At the end of the message, Ana-María leaned over and said, "That sermon was for you, huh?" Funny thing—to this day I can't even remember what he preached on, not a single phrase he said or a Scripture he referenced. As the speaker concluded, he looked to a young woman on his left and said, "I believe we have a word from God today." She stood up with her Bible spread open in her hands and began to read: "For the revelation awaits an appointed time; it speaks of the end and will not prove false. Though it linger, wait for it; it will certainly come and will not delay" (Habakkuk 2:3).

My entire being was shaking as she read the verse. I honestly don't know why God chose to speak to me through a minor prophet like Habakkuk. Why not David? Or Joseph? What about Job? Those guys spent plenty of time in peril and strife. I didn't understand one single bit of it, but there was no doubt in me that God was telling me He had something in store for me. As I let it sink in, I wept profusely. *Something* inside me said there was something bigger ahead and that we would need patience to endure until it arrived. I walked out of that church a different woman—a woman filled with more hope.

God's Faithfulness

After Ana-María and I had lunch together, we went to see a friend of hers. She was a musician, and soon after our arrival we were sitting at the piano and singing together. My heart was still very tender, and within seconds, tears were falling down my face. I proceeded to share with her what was happening in my marriage. She brought comfort to my soul by listening to me without offering any advice or petty words to make me feel better. She did something even better.

She said, "Cindy, I feel like I need to share a verse with you." She left the piano to go get her Bible. When she returned she said, "It says in Habakkuk 2:3 that the revelation awaits an appointed time, it speaks of the end…"

Even as I thought, "Who in the world reads Habakkuk!" I had to acknowledge what was happening. Not only did God deliver my request by giving me a word from His Word, but He did it twice. I'm pretty sure God knew that He'd have to hit me over the head with His message before I'd grab ahold of it with my heart and believe. My heart had been broken by human unfaithfulness, but the way to healing was without a doubt coming from God's unwavering faithfulness.

All I could do after that was praise God for being so sweet to me. Many would think He was late in delivering, but I'm aware that He was right on time.

The Answer that Matters

As I drove back to Georgetown that afternoon, I heard God's voice over and over and over in my head. "Do you trust Me?" I was hesitant to answer Him; I knew what saying yes would mean. It would mean staying in a marriage that was deeply wounded, nearly destroyed. It would mean forgiving a man for breaking his marriage vows over and over again. It would mean remaining in a trustless marriage until Chris could build that trust back up, which may take the rest of his life. But after wrestling in prayer and remembering the promises that God had made to me in His Word, I answered.

I said yes. Through tears, through pain, through heartache…but also through hope.

And no sooner had that word come out of my mouth than God's supernatural, indescribable peace that passes *all* understanding overwhelmed my heart, soul, and mind. That was all God wanted from me. He wanted me to wave the white flag, to throw my hands up in surrender. He wanted me to do that so He could take over. God spoke loud and clear—not once, but twice, in the words of two separate, unsuspecting individuals. The week I spent in Texas proved to be a turning point for me.

The next step would be to trust that this peace and hope that God just poured into me would remain through the night and into the morning. I had received a few hope transplants over the last week, but I was still a little doubtful that the next morning would be any different from the previous 20 mornings. Nevertheless, I moved forward, putting one foot in front of the other, holding out hope that I was beginning a new leg of my journey.

For the first time in three weeks, I awoke from my sleep the next morning without that sick feeling, that awful realization that my old life was over. For some odd and unexplainable reason, I was encouraged that maybe, just maybe something good was on the horizon for our family.

I packed up my SUV, buckled my three-year-old son in his car seat, and headed north toward the Sooner state. I was going home to my husband.

What to Stand On

Finding truths to stand on is vital for our faith life—and never more so than when we have been let down by others, ourselves, and a lack of truth in our lives. You truly do feel out at sea without a paddle, a raft, or a life jacket once lies wash over you and the life you once had. Wisdom from godly people will help you stay afloat, but it will be God's truth that carries you to solid ground, where you have a better perspective, not to mention a safer one!

My trip to Texas had helped redirect me toward God's truths. So after I returned home to Oklahoma, fueled with a bit of hope and an overwhelming sense of being loved by God, I was hungry for even more of His truth for my situation and my life from that day forward.

I was reminded of a trip Chris and I took to Panama City Beach, Florida, with a group of kids from the Tennessee church where Chris was the youth pastor. We and the kids were extremely excited about the event we were attending because one of the featured speakers was Josh McDowell.

Decades ago, McDowell was searching for meaning in life. He had tried religion but was not satisfied. He then set out to prove Christianity false. In pursuit of this goal, he came to the following conclusions about truths we can stand on that are in the Bible.

- Jesus Christ is who He said He was.
- There is historic evidence for the reliability of Scripture.
- The resurrection of Christ took place.[1]

I made the choice to stay in my marriage because of God's Word to me in Habakkuk 2:3, so you can imagine that this knowledge came in handy. It would have been easy for me to just listen to wise counsel and do what others thought I should do—which is exactly why I kept asking God for a word. I know the Word of God is true. I trust it. I believe it. I do my best to live it.

To this day, McDowell's words have provided more stability and clarity for my faith in Christ than anything else I have ever heard. I learned that the Bible was written over a 1500-year span by more than 40 authors in different places in three different languages. I learned that it covered many different topics, many of which are controversial. And despite all of these differences, from Genesis to Revelation the Bible's authors spoke in harmony and with continuity about one unfolding story—God's redemption of man.

I don't completely understand every single part of God's inspired Word, and I don't expect to. God speaks very clearly to Isaiah on that matter: "'For my thoughts are not your thoughts, neither are your ways my ways,' declares the LORD. As the heavens are higher than the earth, so are my ways higher than your ways and my thoughts than your thoughts'" (Isaiah 55:8-9).

Find Your Footing

You may be at a place in life much like where I was some years ago. You may believe in God and read His Word and share about His love with others. I did all that too. But you may not be completely aware of the foundation upon which your faith is built. My hope is that you will continue on a journey to know not only what you believe but also why you believe it. And trust me, there's nothing like having your world torn apart and ripped out from underneath you to get you jump-started.

Is God's Grace Sufficient?

What exactly does it mean that God's grace is sufficient for me? That His power is made perfect in my weakness? Maybe you are famil-iar with this passage:

> To keep me from becoming conceited because of these sur-passingly great revelations, there was given me a thorn in my flesh, a messenger of Satan, to torment me. Three times I pleaded with the Lord to take it away from me. But he said to me, "My grace is sufficient for you, for my power is made perfect in weakness." Therefore I will boast all the more gladly about my weaknesses, so that Christ's power may rest on me. That is why, for Christ's sake, I delight in weaknesses, in insults, in hardships, in persecutions, in difficulties. For when I am weak, then I am strong (2 Corinthians 12:7-10).

I'm far from a theologian, but this does not sound like fun to me *at all*! A thorn in the flesh that won't go away? Ouch. A messenger of Satan? Get out of town!

Before Chris' confession, I must have read that passage a hundred times. I am pretty sure I can quote it without even looking at it. But even though I'd read it and quoted it, I never really got it until I set out to get it. Allow me to explain.

I decided to embark on a little research journey about this passage of Scripture. My first stop was a more recent paraphrase of the Bible that has proven to help people like me understand God's Word better.

> Because of the extravagance of those revelations, and so I wouldn't get a big head, I was given the gift of a handicap to keep me in constant touch with my limitations. Satan's angel did his best to get me down; what he in fact did was push me to my knees. No danger then of walking around high and mighty! At first I didn't think of it as a gift, and begged God to remove it. Three times I did that, and then he told me,
>
>> My grace is enough; it's all you need.
>> My strength comes into its own in your
>>   weakness.
>
> Once I heard that, I was glad to let it happen. I quit focusing on the handicap and began appreciating the gift. It was a case of Christ's strength moving in on my weakness. Now I take limitations in stride, and with good cheer, these limitations that cut me down to size—abuse, accidents, opposition, bad breaks. I just let Christ take over! And so the weaker I get, the stronger I become (MSG).

Reading that version of the passage helped me understand it so much more. Even so, I still needed more clarity on one part: "My grace is sufficient for you." I know what each word in the phrase means individually, but all together they were causing confusion. I had yet to find the words I needed to impart this biblical truth to myself, let alone to others. So I did what any normal person would do when he or she wants to get to the bottom of something she doesn't understand.

I looked it up.

Good old Webster defines *grace* as "unmerited, divine assistance given humans for their regeneration or sanctification." Here is how I reworded the phrase to help me better grasp what God was trying to say to me: "My unmerited, divine assistance given to you is enough."

My effort to gain more insight into this passage of Scripture led me to multiple commentaries. After much reading, I can only conclude that even though Paul prayed that his thorn would be taken from him, God didn't remove it but gave Paul the strength to endure it. Oftentimes, God works that way. We may not be spared from hardships, pain, or difficulties, but His strength is enough to help us conquer them.

God's unmerited, divine assistance is enough. Period. It's enough when things are going great and the stars are aligned, and it's enough when God chooses to allow something dreadful to come across your path. It's enough. It's not easy, but it is what we need. And praise God for that.

Expect Grace for the Unexpected

I often feel uncomfortable when people approach me with accolades that I feel I don't deserve. Many are in awe that I could have remained in my marriage to a man who hurt me so deeply. Others find it encouraging that I was willing to risk my heart yet again in order to make my marriage work. It's as if people think I was a pillar of strength from the beginning. I wasn't. I'm still not. I am secure in my new life and relationship with Chris, but it took some time to get to this place.

I didn't think my life would turn out like this. I never imagined that someday, at my 20-year high school reunion, I'd tell people that my marriage almost ended due to infidelity and that I have three boys, but the one in the middle lives with his momma in another state. How's that for a conversation starter? There are many things I would like to change about my life, but I don't spend too much time dwelling on that. The past is the past. No sense crying over something that is done. Accept it. Learn from it. Grieve it. Move on. That's how I roll.

God didn't spare me infidelity. He didn't spare me pain even though I interceded on behalf of my husband and marriage for years. I went through some unnecessary pain and humiliation that could have been avoided had my husband dealt with his addiction and sought true help. So what. I learned that all humans are capable of sinning in ways they never imagined, and I lost some faith in mankind. Next, please.

I also learned that what God says in His Word, the inspired Holy Bible, is absolutely, without a doubt, true. That He really does take ashes and make something beautiful from them. That He really does rain down His peace, which passes understanding, when you pray and petition Him in all things. That He really can use the power of a testimony to bring those far from Him into a relationship with Him.

Is His grace sufficient?

You bet yer bottom dollar it is.

Your Healing Journey

1. Where do you go or to whom do you run when trouble crosses your path?

2. Do you believe God speaks to His people through His Word? Has He ever spoken to you in that way?

3. Is God's grace enough to get you through your circumstance? If not, how can you get to a place where you believe it is?

4. Have you asked God to lead you in your situation? Have you come to Him with your hurts and needs and hopes? Do this now. Pray and watch for God's leading to come into your life.

4

Learning to Cope

YOUR ROAD TO RESTORATION might take different turns from mine, but I can tell you that it will begin the very same way: by putting one foot in front of the other and keeping your focus on what needs to be done today and what your hope is for tomorrow.

One of our first steps was to do things again as a family. This decision to be united in tasks and fun activities started moving us forward. Things were on the mend, and we were communicating better than we ever had. We had some really good days, but there were also some really bad days.

Fear of Not Being Enough

God had indeed done heart surgery on me while I was in Texas, but I was still struggling with the fact that my husband got another woman pregnant. Every time I would go there in my mind, I was crushed. Crushed because when I said my wedding vows to my husband and he said his to me, forsaking all others was part of the deal. I was absolutely on board with that. My declaration of my love for him proved just that. I didn't need—or for that matter, want—another man in my life. Chris Beall was enough. But as we walked the next month out, I couldn't help but wonder if I was enough for him. He assured me that I was enough and that his acting out sexually was due to his pornography addiction. It wasn't my fault.

Still, I couldn't help but wonder if there was something I could have done differently. Maybe I could have been skinnier, blonder, nicer, funnier...dare I say it, even a little naughtier in the bedroom. Would that have worked for him? Would that have kept him from cheating on me?

Battling that issue was something I truly did: battle. I spent days on end wondering what was wrong with me. Finally, it dawned on me that nothing was wrong with me. I wasn't claiming perfection by any means, but as Chris disclosed more information about his addiction, I realized that he was addicted even during the days when I was pleased with myself physically. The days when I could put on a bikini and not even have to hold my abs in. The days when everything was in place and completely perked up, if you know what I mean. So as I pushed through this pain with him, I began to slowly free myself from this unnecessary burden that I put on myself. But it was far from easy. It was a daily, mental battle that I faced and that I still face today.

Everything We Need

When I think about how I had to transform my mind in lasting ways, I can't help but think about Moses. Here's a guy whom God called to lead the Israelites out from under Pharaoh's regime. He has to go to Pharaoh and demand freedom for his people, and then he has to convince his people, the Israelites, that he is indeed for them.

But see, Moses has this issue. He doesn't feel good about himself and definitely thinks that someone else would be a better fit for the job. In the fourth chapter of Exodus, we hear Moses pleading with the Lord after he's been given specific instructions about the next steps to take.

"O Lord, I have never been eloquent, neither in the past not since you have spoken to your servant. I am slow of speech and tongue."

The LORD said to him, "Who gave man his mouth? Who makes him deaf or mute? Who gives him sight or makes him blind? Is it not I, the LORD? Now go; I will help you speak and will teach you what to say."

But Moses said, "O Lord, please send someone else to do it" (Exodus 4:10-13).

Really, Moses? You heard the Creator of the universe tell you that He will help you speak and teach you what to say, and you are still begging God to send someone else to do the job that He has clearly laid out for you?

We are like that too, you know. God may not have called us to lead His people from captivity under a vicious ruler like Pharaoh, but He has spoken His truth to us through His inspired Word, and we still don't believe it. We don't believe that "[God] has given us everything we need for life and godliness through our knowledge of him who called us by his own glory and goodness" (2 Peter 1:3).

Instead we choose to believe the lies of this world. We don't see that "man looks at the outward appearance, but God looks at the heart" (1 Samuel 16:7).

I know this stuff backward, forward, sideways, and backward again. I preach it, I exhort with it, I read about it…but honestly, I don't know that my belief has hit the crisis point just yet. Oh, I so want it to. I want to be the kind of woman who is more concerned about her inward beauty than about having enough money saved up for a new pair of jeans for the fall.

So please hear my heart in this. I'm not scolding you by any means. I am simply saying that we must come to a place in our lives where we truly believe that what God, our Sustainer, says about us is more influential in our lives than what we see on any billboard.

Working Through the Aftermath

My husband's infidelity wasn't about me. It wasn't my fault. I know this. But it is easy to get lost in misunderstandings about how trust is broken and how problems arise in a marriage.

I did still ask myself questions because I know that marriages don't fail entirely because of one person. Sure, one person may be doing more of the negative stuff than the other, but as I've always said, "It takes two to make a marriage work and two to make it fail."

So although I definitely don't believe it was my fault, I do feel it was only right for me to begin asking questions: Did I do anything to contribute to this mess? Was there something I could have done differently? Questions like these can help us maintain a humble and teachable spirit.

Even though I had heard from God and now had my hope restored, these gifts didn't take away all the pain. I still had to deal with the mental images of my husband with other women. The pain I felt as I battled mentally during that season was tremendous. At times I could almost feel blood dripping from my broken heart. Sometimes I couldn't even find my breath.

At the same time, I trusted God. I wasn't without hope. I was grieving the loss of something I didn't deserve to lose, but I was not hopeless. I was confused and perplexed, but I was not throwing in the towel. My heart was postured for redemption, and I was willing to endure whatever was necessary to save my marriage, even if it hurt like crazy. Which it did.

The Physical Consequences

Committing adultery is not only spiritually wrong but also can bring dire physical implications. My husband was unemployed, so we had no health insurance. But we needed to look into some things that a lot of people would rather just sweep under the rug. Apparently, having an "out of sight, out of mind" thought pattern is rather popular when it comes to something like this. But I needed to know if my husband's irresponsible actions had caused any physical harm to either of our bodies. I needed to know if he had contracted or given me any sexually transmitted diseases. Gulp.

I had never set foot in a county health department. Honestly, I never had a reason to. Until then.

Below is my journal entry for March 1, 2002. I wrote it after my visit to the health department. In no way do I mean for my words to be offensive to anyone in any demographic or life circumstance. These are my gut-wrenching feelings. I started out on this journey inviting you to feel every emotion with me. I don't intend to stop now.

> The consequences of Chris' actions began to be revealed to us both. The realist in me knew that we both needed to be tested for sexually transmitted diseases...especially HIV. And just to add insult to injury, we were without health insurance. So we proceeded to go to the health department because the testing was free of charge. It was heart wrenching and completely humiliating going to "that place." The company there was not what I was accustomed to. I wondered how many were prostitutes or drug dealers. I wanted to shout, "I DO NOT BELONG HERE! I AM A PASTOR'S WIFE!" But by the looks on the faces of the people surrounding me, that was the last thing they cared about.

I'll never forget that day. After waiting by myself in a rather dirty lobby area, I was called back to an examination room. After getting undressed and prepared for my medical visit, I was greeted by a doctor. I use the term *greeted* very loosely. Her entrance into the room was anything but warm. She wasn't necessarily rude to me, just very matter-of-fact. And when you are a caregiver and strong feeler like I am, matter-of-fact encounters crush you deeply.

The examination was not pleasant. After that visit, I realized just how great a visit to my gynecologist was. At least my OB-GYN actually smiled at me and talked to me as he examined my body. Not a single word was said to me by this doctor. I can't really pass judgment because

I don't know what her life is like. But her manner added to my humil-iation and sense of loneliness.

Once we were finished, I got dressed and waited for her to return. She came back in and let me know that I might have a particular STD called chlamydia. I know she saw the look on my face change. As if it could get any worse. But it did, and I began to cry. (Not the ugly cry, but definitely tears flowing down my face.) I don't know if she just didn't have it in her to be sympathetic toward me or if she'd seen so much of this that it had numbed her. Whatever the case, I felt alone and abandoned in a moment of true need. And I wanted to tell her that this was not my fault. I wasn't the one sleeping around unprotected. I was faithful and true and honest and striving to be a godly, honorable wife and mom. I'm certain that my sharing that with her would have only been for my benefit. She truly didn't care.

I left the building with tears streaming down my face. I walked into our home with my heart and pride in a million pieces. Chris' heart sank as he watched me crumble in front of him, and he began to apologize profusely. The upside was that I learned this STD could be treated with antibiotics. However, just knowing that I might have this condition was so painful and awful. I felt dirty. I didn't deserve this.

The Agony of Waiting

Three weeks after we both made our first humiliating trip to the county health department, we returned. It wasn't something I desired to do, but in order to get the results of our HIV test, we had to be physically present. We'd driven down there with Noah sitting in the backseat. Chris held my hand the whole way there and made frequent glances my way. I must have just been staring straight ahead, convinc-ing myself that everything would be fine.

In just a few moments, we were both going to learn about our future. It took everything in me to battle the questions that kept forc-ing themselves into my mind: Will I be alive to raise Noah? If I have HIV, will people shun me? How will I handle the pain and discomfort that this deadly disease brings? Will my mother ever be able to forgive the man whose actions killed her baby girl?

Chris felt obligated to go in to receive his results first while I waited in the car with Noah. He told me that if he was the one who sentenced me to long-term illness and possible death, he wanted to learn about it first. Despite his actions that put us in this circumstance in the first place, his actions since his confession day had been honorable.

The wait in the car was excruciating. I was trying to preoccupy myself by answering the questions my three-year-old was asking. All the while, I stared at the entrance to the building, hoping to see my husband exit while jumping up and down, which would have been a sure sign that he was not infected.

Infected. What an unclean word. But it was the only suitable one to describe our current situation. Either he was or he wasn't. Either he infected me or he didn't.

There was no jumping up and down or dancing around by my husband as he came out of the building, but as he approached our car, I saw him smile at me and shake his head no. I was only partially relieved, for I still had to go in to get my results. As you can guess, they were also negative. Neither of us was infected with HIV.

Not only did I learn that I wasn't HIV positive that day, I also learned that I was not infected with chlamydia. I did experience some relief with those results, but the process to get there was stunningly painful. I wouldn't wish it on my worst enemy.

Getting the confirmation we needed about our physical well-being literally gave us a new lease on life. It was as if we were both holding our breath for weeks, wondering if trying to make our marriage work was even worth the effort. I mean, you can't make your marriage work if you know you're going to die. It was definitely a good day to rejoice.

Financial Survival

One of the things we had to get in place was a way to earn money. Part of our healing and restoration process included being shepherded by the church leadership. And that meant that if we wanted their assistance, support, love, and guidance, we basically did what they recommended. What they recommended was that Chris find a job where there would be no travel involved and no Internet, which in our day could be quite a challenge.

We actually didn't have to look long before God's provision found us. One thing I have always admired about my husband is his willingness to provide for his family. He wasn't one of those men who thought a certain type of job was beneath him. He didn't care. He is an incredibly handy man who can fix almost anything or at least figure out a way to get it done. Because of that, I encouraged him to apply at The Home Depot. At first he wasn't sure he wanted to, but eventually he did. Within a month of leaving the LifeChurch.tv staff, he was selling two-by-fours to local contractors.

You don't always know what kind of man you married until you see him go through difficulties. My husband had just endured one of the most humiliating things a man can go through, and yet he woke up every morning at 5:30 to go make $10 an hour for his family. And he did it with a smile on his face because we were still with him.

I also happened to land a part-time job at, of all places, LifeChurch.tv. God showed Himself by providing something right up my alley. That job was indeed a blessing and part of God's provision for our family, but it was incredibly humiliating to walk in the first day to that job. I wondered what everyone was thinking. Were they having pity on me because of the confession my husband made? Were they talking about me behind my back? Did they think I got hired just because everyone felt sorry for me? Did they think I was a fool for staying with a man who had fooled me? Would he fool me again?

People were definitely nice to me, but they were also very careful around me. It was as if there was some big, blue elephant in the room that nobody knew how to walk around. But they tried. A few were brave enough to tell me to my face that they believed in us and were praying for us. The rest just went about their quiet ways and prayed silently for us. I know they did. I could see it on their faces. Regardless, it was still difficult to walk into a building where everyone knew our business. *All* of our business.

But it was also one of the most freeing experiences I had. There was no gossip. There was no wondering what happened. Everyone knew.

Desperate for Normal

The biggest despair I experienced in these days came from the knowledge that a baby would soon be born. This part of our story hurt me more deeply than any other part. Yes, it was difficult when I thought about my husband giving himself to other women. But knowing that a child would forever be in our lives and that his presence would always remind us of these painful days—that often sent me over the edge.

Because of this, I wanted some sort of normalcy in my life. I wanted to experience things that other people experienced every day. I didn't want my life to stay in this holding pattern that it seemed to be in. I craved things that took my mind off of my circumstances. Mindless sitcoms, five-year-old movies on one of our seven TV channels, taking my son to the park after getting a slush from Sonic. Whatever I could do to get my mind off it, I did. I had to do it. I needed to do it.

But as much as I tried or wanted to forget about the circumstances looming over me, I soon found out that normal, as I knew it, was over. I had to find my new normal. This new normal of mine included a past of infidelity and a dead marriage. This new normal would include another child whom I did not bring into this world. This new normal would include a ton of things that I never imagined when I dreamed about having a man sweep me off my feet.

I already told you how I believe God called me to stay and fight for my marriage. I know many still wonder why I didn't leave and how I could have truly stayed. People think I'm a doormat. People think I'm a fool. People think I'm taking a risk that is going to backfire. Perhaps. But it is a risk I took willingly because I trust my God.

After all, He's the only One who has never let me down.

Your Healing Journey

1. As you pick up the pieces of your broken world, what are some of the things you are doing? In which areas are you feeling stuck? How might you get unstuck?

2. Do you ever find yourself struggling to believe the truth about who God says you are? What do you do when that happens? Who in your life speaks truth about your value as a loved child of God? If nobody is currently doing this, ask God to connect you to someone who can shed light on your identity in Christ and your worth as His child.

3. If you've ever gone through a humiliating situation like Cindy's, what character traits did you see come out in you? In what way were you surprised? *I never expected to stay in a marriage with these circumstances.*

4. Can you relate to Cindy when she said she had to find her new normal? What does your new normal look and feel like? If you aren't there yet, what do you hope will be a part of your new normal?

Our new normal ... a much simpler life, less material things, spending less money, focused on rebuilding our relationship and protecting it, church groups, friends, helping others,

5. How do you feel about Cindy's statement about God—"He's the only one who has never let me down"? Do you believe that to be true in your life? Why or why not? *Sometimes I have felt that God has let me down because of the unfair situation I am in because of mikes choices. However, mikes choices are not God's fault. God is the only one to redeem our marriage and our only hope to make it "better than new".*

A Story of Healing in Their Own Words

BRIAN AND JENNI

I HAVE YET TO MEET BRIAN AND JENNI. I have been a blog friend of Jenni's for quite some time now. I'm inspired by her transparency as she shared their story because Jenni is the one who was unfaithful. It takes an incredibly strong person to be willing to let her flaws be made known to the entire world—or at least those who choose to read about it on the Internet.

Brian and Jenni are just a few years into their story, but I think you'll hear from their words that God has brought about healing at a rapid rate. These two are crazy cool and truly exhibit the "whatever it takes" mind-set. You can read more about their story on Jenni's blog at www .jenniclayville.com.

CINDY: Brian, what was your initial response when you found out about Jenni's infidelity?

BRIAN: It was one of complete shock and confusion. I was sad, hurt, and confused. My anger did not kick in for a couple of days.

CINDY: Jenni, did you ever think you'd do such a thing as commit adultery?

JENNI: I *never* thought I'd commit adultery. Yet when I decided to have an affair, I literally decided to. I knew what I was doing while

I was in it. I gave away a piece of my heart to a man who was not my husband. Did I feel bad? Yes. Did it stop me? No.

CINDY: Brian, did you ever consider getting a divorce?

BRIAN: I didn't really try to tackle the question of staying married immediately. I did think seriously of leaving several times. I love my boys and wanted them to have a stable two-parent home to grow up in. Over time it was clear that Jenni was totally committed to our marriage and me. I knew as we worked through counseling that I really loved her. I wanted to beat the odds. Many people were praying for us, and God was walking with me on the really hard days when I couldn't do it alone.

CINDY: Jenni, how have you dealt with the pain you've seen in Brian's eyes over the years?

JENNI: I'll never forget the pain in his eyes when I first told him. I'll never forget holding my breath and watching his responses as I answered his questions about time, places, occurrences, and other specifics. I was just waiting for him to say, "This is too much! You've gone too far! I want a divorce!" But he never did. I prayed for a new heart. I prayed for patience because I knew the healing process could take years. I had already decided I would spend the rest of my life trying to make right what I had wronged. I knew I needed to give back more than what I had wrongfully taken.

CINDY: Brian, how have you been able to forgive Jenni?

BRIAN: Knowing that Jenni was completely repentant and that she cut off all communication with the other man helped me heal. I completely looked to God for the strength to fully forgive Jenni. It took time, and it was a very deliberate choice. When I asked God to help me find permanent forgiveness, He asked me how much I have been forgiven by Him. As I processed this question, it suddenly became clear to me that the only way I could live with no bitterness in my marriage was to forgive and move forward. That day I experienced the sweetest peace from the Lord, and I came home excited to tell Jenni that I could finally forgive and know that I fully meant it.

CINDY: Jenni, do you ever find yourself walking in shame because of what you did?

JENNI: Yes. Sometimes I find myself back in that shameful place. I'm still disappointed in my past decision...that will probably never change. I *know* I've been forgiven—not only by Brian, but by God. I even forgive myself on most days. To say I'm over it would almost be like saying I haven't learned my lesson. It's the conviction of my past choices that keep me from repeating them. I won't be forgetting my mistake anytime soon, but I don't live in my past.

CINDY: What about trust?

BRIAN: She has made trusting her very easy for me. She gave me access to all her social media and e-mail accounts. She does not spend time with any male friends alone, and she has created very big boundaries around her to show that she is committed to not repeating her mistake. We have talked about anything that makes me a little uncomfortable, and she is careful to respect my concerns.

JENNI: I am not defensive when my integrity is questioned. If it's questioned, it's because it should be. But if I'm innocent, I don't have to defend myself because those closest to me will do it for me. My life is to be lived above reproach.

CINDY: When you look at Brian now, how does it make you feel?

JENNI: Lucky. Fortunate. Passionately in love. Passionately loved. Blessed. Free. Forgiven. Restored.

CINDY: How is your marriage today?

BRIAN: Healthy, happy, growing, discovering. For the first time, I feel like we both understand who we are as individuals and how to love each other as we are. We have a much deeper spiritual connection with open lines of communication about everything. The more we pursue a spiritual life together, really praying and talking about what God is saying to us, the more we feel connected. We have not arrived, but we are to a place where we are enjoying the growing process.

JENNI: Our marriage has never been better. I've never been more certain that Brian is exactly the man God created for me. Our marriage is exciting and fulfilling. I feel like there's still so much about Brian I'm getting to learn about. But at the same time, our marriage is comfortable and familiar…like my favorite pair of jeans. This all comes from communication. We decided to divorce our old marriage and start a new one. Our new marriage has some talking, but much more listening, watching, and trusting. This is communication.

5

He Didn't Plan It

On January 9, 1993, Chris and I were about to become husband and wife. The Texas temps were in the low seventies, and the entire wedding party was in shorts. When I glanced down at my hand that would soon bear a wedding ring, the fresh acrylic nails made me laugh. I knew that within 48 hours, I'd have them yanked off my tomboy hands. But everything else felt real and wonderful.

Chris and I had decided to sidestep tradition and see each other before our ceremony began. We spent a tender few minutes praying together. We gently held hands and could barely speak because we were in awe that the day we'd been anticipating for months was coming to pass. And we were ready to head down that aisle toward our "ever after."

When it came time for the vows, we went the way of tradition because we planned to keep these words of covenant all of our days. As the ceremony closed with Chris' father singing "The Lord's Prayer" a cappella, we looked at each other with delight and excitement, ready to begin our life together.

When the Vow Breaks

The vows we said to each other that day were our proclamation of love and devotion. You've been to plenty of weddings, I'm sure. We could all probably recite those traditional vows from memory…"for better or for worse, for richer or for poorer, in sickness and in health… to love and to cherish from this day forward until death do us part." The words were simple but meaningful.

But that shiny, joyful moment of exchanging vows before God and our family and friends cast greater shadows over the news six years later because my knight in shining armor chose to walk the road of unfaithfulness. This truth not only stunned me but also shocked everyone in our lives, including those who shared in the joy of our journey's beginning. Many would say, "Chris Beall would never do such a thing. He is a pastor, for cryin' out loud. He shares Jesus with people. He leads God's people in worship each Sunday. He's an anointed man of God!" Have you had those thoughts over the years when certain moral scandals have hit the news or at least become well-known in smaller circles? I know I have.

Most people don't plan to commit such gross acts of sin. Over the years, Chris and I have met with many couples who are living out the consequences of being unfaithful. And you know how many of the adulterers said they planned to do it?

Nada. Zilch. Zero.

Not a single person said, "Yeah, I figured that around year four or seven or eighteen, I would go ahead and commit adultery, break the heart of my spouse, lose the respect and admiration of my children, and absolutely wreck my future." It just doesn't happen that way 99.9 percent of the time.

Sin: It Ain't Nothin' New

King David is someone we can see fall into sin. Tumble is more like it. Maybe you've read the story of his bad choice in 2 Samuel 11. Allow me to paraphrase.

It was springtime. Most kings from other kingdoms had gone off to war, but David made the decision to stay home. He must have been experiencing insomnia because one night he got up from his bed and went out on the roof. When he did this, he saw a beautiful woman bathing across the way. Captivated by her loveliness and probably more than a little turned on, he sent someone to find out about her. Big mistake number one.

Now, one might hope that as soon as David found out that she was married to Uriah, one of his best warriors, he would just let the whole thing go. Not so much. David sent his messengers to get her and bring her to him. Big mistake number two. Upon her arrival, he must have made it known to her what he wanted. The Bible is clear that they had sexual intercourse before she went back home. Biggest mistake of all.

I don't think David had any plan whatsoever to commit adultery with Bathsheba that day, which clearly illustrates the point of this chapter. I believe this because the Bible says that David was a man after God's own heart (1 Samuel 13:14). He was also the kind of king who chose to show favor to the house of Saul, the crazy king before him who tried to take David's life, by asking in 2 Samuel 9:1, "Is there anyone still left of the house of Saul to whom I can show kindness for Jonathan's sake?" Clearly, David was an honorable man whose heart was to honor the one true God even when a crazy, deranged king was chasing him all over the country.

Not only that, but as David defeated the Philistines and Moabites (and a whole lot of other "ites"), he dedicated to the Lord all the victories and the articles he acquired.

I don't know if you realized this part of the story, but David's decision to stay home and not go off to war was on the heels of some pretty awesome victories. Victories, as I mentioned above, that were followed by David worshipping and honoring God after he was awarded the trophy.

Isn't that just like our spiritual enemy? He often plans his attack right after something amazing has happened in our lives or after we've been a part of making something amazing happen in our lives or in the lives of others. He does this because we are not on our guard to protect our hearts and relationships from his schemes. This is the time that we relax and sit back with the "Oh, I'd never do that to my spouse" mind-set. And before people realize that they've crossed lines that they never thought they would, they are in someone else's bed doing things that are only supposed to be done with their spouse.

The story of David and Bathsheba is the perfect confirmation of the phrase, "Idle hands are the devil's workshop," wouldn't you say? I mean, he was home at the time when other kings had gone off to war. He was up in his room in his bed and couldn't sleep. I bet if he had been fighting in wars and leading his country in battle, he'd have been sleeping soundly that night. I find myself thinking that if he had done what he was supposed to do, the whole fiasco with Bathsheba wouldn't have happened.

But it did. And we can learn from it.

Never Say Never

After hearing my story, you might think that it would be highly unlikely that I would ever cheat on my husband. If someone said to you, "I just heard Cindy Beall had an affair," you would probably be shocked, right? But I know otherwise.

I know that one slight step off the narrow road I'm called to walk could lead me down a path of temptation and eventual regret. One deep, disclosing conversation could start an unhealthy relationship with an old friend. One haughty "I'm above such a sin" mind-set could bring about more devastation to my husband and sons than I believe I am capable of handling. And honestly, it scares the living daylights out of me.

I know me, and I know that sometimes I feed my flesh and discard my spirit. Also, I've had too many discussions with people who wound up doing things they never imagined doing. I wonder if you've said you'd never do something, only to find yourself doing the thing you said you'd never do.

Like the young woman who told her husband just last week that she kissed another man and never dreamed that she'd ever do such a thing.

Or the 55-year-old husband, father, and grandfather, the longtime epitome of marital faithfulness, who ditched his wife for a younger woman. "He'd never do such a thing," his friends said about him.

I don't believe I live a life of fear, but I do believe I have a healthy, God-fearing attitude that will help me make choices now before I'm thrown into a circumstance that I didn't see coming. I know that my spiritual enemy "prowls around like a roaring lion looking for someone to devour" (1 Peter 5:8), so I am usually on my guard. Some might say I'm focusing on the negative too much. Perhaps. But after what I've been through in my marriage, I know what can happen.

I am fully aware that when we fail to plan, we plan to fail. And trust me when I say this: I'm not planning to be unfaithful. I'm planning not to.

We Aren't Immune

In 2002, shortly after Chris' confession to me, Beth Moore released a book that I picked up. I'd been a student of hers since my midtwenties and have enjoyed the books and studies she's written.

Reading this book, *When Godly People Do Ungodly Things*, turned out to be a monumental step toward my healing. I knew it was more than a coincidence that this book was released so close to the date of Chris' confession.

Needless to say, I grabbed the book and dove in. I drank in the contents like a woman dying of thirst. I spent a lot of time nodding my head in agreement with Beth as I read the truth she wrote. I allowed myself to weep as I recounted some of the pain I'd recently endured.

I think what ministered to me most from her book was the knowledge that I wasn't alone. She basically said that there are countless Christ followers out there who are falling into habitual sin.

Not only can the godly suddenly sprawl into a ditch from a solid, upright path, I believe many are. I am convinced, as the days, weeks, and months blow off the Kingdom calendar, that the casualties are growing in number by harrowing leaps and bounds. Many just aren't talking because they are scared half to death. Not so much of God as they are of the church. To say that the body of Christ would be shocked to know how bloody and bruised by defeat they are is a gross understatement. Among the better pieces of news is that God is most assuredly not shocked. Grieved perhaps, but not shocked. You see, He told us this was coming.[2]

When Chris and I went public with our story, what we'd known in our hearts truly came to pass. We weren't the only ones whose marriage had suffered from pornography and sexual addiction. I can't count the number of couples who approached my husband, asking for guidance, wisdom, and encouragement as they were beginning their painful journey. Many of them chose to face it and endure it only because of the strength, humility, and vulnerability that my husband showed.

Those Whom God Uses

Beginning to voice our story publicly brought about questions from many. Can God really still use Chris Beall? Doesn't the Bible say he has lost his chance? Apparently God does use imperfect people. (Who knew?)

He chose to use the apostle Paul, an upstanding, fine, law-abiding Pharisee, as one of His instruments to speak truth to us through many New Testament writings. But at one time, Paul was famous for persecuting followers of Christ. Then, somewhere along the road on a trip to Damascus, Paul's eyes got burned. Blinded by the light, he could not make the rest of the journey without help. He heard some instructions from Christ and made his way toward Ananias to get healed. After his encounter with the Living God, he became a man who lived to tell others about Jesus. Quite a transformation, isn't it? This fact alone proves that our God is fully willing to use anyone to accomplish His will.

Paul wrote about false apostles in his second letter to the church in Corinth. He was concerned about the believers being led astray. "But I am afraid that just as Eve was deceived by the serpent's cunning, your minds may somehow be led astray from your sincere and pure devotion to Christ" (2 Corinthians 11:3).

You see, many people think that Christ followers aren't subject to such gross sin. They don't expect really strong believers to fall the way my husband did. They expect perfection. But Paul is very clear that even those who are sincerely and purely devoted to Christ can fall. And they often do.

So what does that look like? What do we do to make sure we don't fall into gross sin in our lives? I definitely have my issues to wade through, but now might be an appropriate time for you to hear from my husband about his addiction to pornography, which is what led him down the road of adultery many years ago.

A Story of Falling, in My Own Words (by Chris Beall)

I am still tender, still amazed that I haven't lost my family, and overwhelmed that I get to serve a leader, Craig Groeschel, who took a huge risk in bringing me back into full-time ministry. But mostly I am speechless because when I look into Cindy's eyes, there is life, hope, and love. We are crazy about each other.

I want to briefly speak to an issue that some of you may be curious about or potentially living through. How does a person become addicted to porn and succumb to having multiple affairs, fathering a child with another woman, and creating an entire second life?

To answer this I want to challenge an assertion that a good friend of mine made this week. He believes this struggle is a symptom of a man not being satisfied at home. I agree that there are some situations in which this is the case. Scripture is clear that husbands and wives are to refrain from sex only when it is a mutual decision and only for specified reasons so that no one would be tempted to sin sexually (1 Corinthians 7:5-9). However, this had absolutely nothing to do with my struggle.

I saw my first *Playboy* when I was young. I can still remember the explicit images I saw in that magazine more than 30 years ago. At that moment, a door of weakness was opened, a door that my spiritual adversary would methodically exploit in the coming years. I do believe that in my situation, porn was not the end to anything, but a symptom of something deeper. I was sexually satisfied at home, yet I consistently and progressively filled my mind with pornographic images. What was my disease? I had grown to believe a lie about who I was.

Now, before you write me off for giving you an ambiguous spiritual answer as the cause of my sexual addiction, I want you to ask yourself this question: Why does anyone sin? Why does someone who is a follower of Christ consistently commit acts of commission or acts of omission that are clearly out of line with God's standard?

For years and years my life and choices reflected a strong disbelief in who God says I am as a follower of Christ. Think about it for a minute. If we all truly believed with everything in us that we are God's workmanship, the righteousness of God in Christ, chosen by Him for works of ministry, seated with Christ in the heavenly realms, and completely accepted and forgiven, would we continue to live consistently and progressively in sin? I am not suggesting that we can become sinless in our daily lives, but it is extremely hard to live in such blatant and growing rebellion to God when we truly believe in who He is and who He says we are in Christ.

How did that play out for me? For years I struggled with accepting God's forgiveness for my sin, and at the same time, I deeply desired the approval of people. I needed the affirmation of others aside from Cindy. Why? Because I really didn't believe that God accepted me as I was. And part of me thought that Cindy's love for me was just because she was married to me. This is where the progression happened. Looking at those images made me feel (for lack of a less cheesy phrase) like a man. Deep down, many guys wrestle with the questions, do I measure up? Do I have what it takes? Am I respected and successful?

When I felt like a failure, I looked to a counterfeit source of validation on the Internet. No addiction is static; it will always progress from one thing to another. If a shot of tequila gives you a buzz, drink one shot every day and see if it still has the same effect after a year. Chances are, you will need progressively more tequila to feel the way you felt that first time. The same is true for people who like the adrenaline rush of extreme or dangerous activities. They provide a mental high, an escape that becomes harder and harder to duplicate because the body and mind become accustomed to each level of excitement, and they crave more.

This is the nature of a sexual addiction. You look at an image and then a video. Then you start chatting with people who have the same struggles, and one day you wake up wondering how on earth you got there. Sin always progresses. Always.

If you are battling something, if you find that you are sinning in the same areas over and over again, chances are that you believe a lie about who God says you are.

He wants to set you free. Free indeed.

Your Healing Journey

1. Can you think of a time you did something bad that you thought you'd never do? (It can be something simple or huge.) How did you justify it at the time or afterward?

2. Do you agree that the church has a harder time accepting a fallen Christian than God does? Do you have a hard time accepting the weaknesses and sins of others? How can you seek to have God's heart for those people who hurt you or others with their behavior?

3. If you've been hurt in your marriage by your spouse's actions, do you think he or she planned to do this?

4. Do you believe God still uses people who have lived in ongoing sin? Share some examples with your group or write down on paper some of those turnaround stories.

6

Finding a Way
Back to Life

I CHOSE TO STAY IN MY MARRIAGE and forgive my husband, but that doesn't mean I was a fool. A lot of people probably thought this about me, but God and I know the whole truth. I was keenly aware that making this choice was a huge risk that could cause my heart to disintegrate should Chris act out again. Yet however dangerous this path might be, I knew it was the one for me. I knew beyond a shadow of a doubt that God wanted to do something with our pain. I just didn't know what. Yet.

I suppose the biggest thing I had to learn to do was get on with my life. I had heard from God and knew what He was calling me to do, but the pain was still there. The broken vows, the loss of trust, and the absolute dread of the mental pictures all occupied my mind daily.

But despite my pain and how bad it hurt, I chose to cling to the little bit of hope I had—the hope given to me by the One who makes all things new. I chose to live by faith. Psalm 27:13 says, "I am still confident of this: I will see the goodness of the LORD in the land of the living."

The word *will* is key here. When King David wrote this, he made a choice to remain confident and trust that he would see the goodness of God. I also made a choice to trust, to walk in faith even when I had no idea where the path would take me and what the terrain would be like along the way. I had to choose to put one foot in front of the other. And so do you.

Let's Give 'Em Something to Talk About

I'll never forget the day we went back to church after Chris' confession. The week prior, Craig shared our story with our LifeChurch.tv campus. We weren't there in person but heard the message later in the day. I don't remember everything he said, but I remember Craig telling the people that the Christian church is the only organization that shoots its wounded. And then he added, "But we're not going to do that." He said the church was going to be a hospital and the people there were going to bring us back to life and watch God make our marriage better than new.

Chris and I were both crying as we walked into the church building. I've not been through anything else quite as humiliating and humbling in my entire life and would prefer that it be kept that way. I mean, come on. As we sat there before the service, a handful of the many caring people came up to us. When Craig came in to preach, he made a comment about our being there. The people erupted in applause, showing their support and love for us. Support and love they said they'd provide to us as we healed. And that is exactly what that group of people did. I couldn't be more grateful.

Sweating the Small Stuff

I found myself going back and forth between extreme hope and awful sadness. Hope was always present, but sometimes I couldn't make it out because of the sadness. The sadness wasn't as deep as it was in the beginning, but it still showed up periodically to disrupt whatever I was doing at the time. I imagine you've been there at some point.

What do you do when you don't want to get out of bed in the

morning but you have people to care for and lists of stuff to do? How do you juggle simple things like laundry, work, caring for your children, and partnering with your spouse when it is impossible for you to trust anything he says, let alone be his biggest supporter?

You do whatever you can in the early days. You cry a lot, which is completely appropriate because you are grieving a loss. You will sometimes have to leave the room because everyone's eyes will be on you, and the discomfort will be more than you can bear. You'll need the prayers of your friends. But even through your tears, you have to find ways to laugh and enjoy life with those closest to you. You have to declare that even though this circumstance might have taken you down, it will not *keep* you down. The bottom line is that you have to choose to cross over and embrace life even as you are mourning the loss of your previous life. I know this well.

Take This Cup, Please

As we worked on making our family of three as wonderful as possible, the reminder that a baby would soon be born was always in the back of my mind. Five months into our healing process, the baby was born. The news broke my heart again. There was no DNA test at this time to prove Chris was the father, but I was fairly certain he was. That is probably what pained me the most—knowing that my husband had a child with another woman.

Six months later, we still had not met the baby, who was named Ben. Chris and I were talking on a cold January afternoon, and our conversation inevitably went to Ben and his mother, Michelle. Chris had begun talking about the baby a little more and discussing our future with him. Times like this sent me over the edge emotionally. It was still so fresh to me, and because of that, I usually ended up in tears. This particular day, I not only began to cry but even left the house and went for a walk—in freezing temperatures and Oklahoma wind. As I walked around my block, tears streaming down my face, I began to bargain with God.

"Please don't let Chris be the father!" I begged.

"My grace is sufficient for you," God gently replied to my heart.

"I can't handle this pain! I don't want to walk this road! I do not deserve this!" I demanded as if I had some sort of authority.

"It's not about you, Cindy." God's words were like spiritual sandpaper.

"I just can't do this. It's too hard, Lord. It hurts too bad," I said with a defeated yet softened spirit.

"*My* grace is sufficient for you. *My* power is going to be made perfect in your weakness." This was God's final reply to me on that dreary afternoon.

I walked back into our warm home, fell to my knees, and wept uncontrollably in my husband's arms. Moved to tears, he held me and just allowed me to grieve over what I didn't deserve to lose. Chris listened intently as I told him about the conversation I had with God on my walk. After a few hours of digesting the encounter I experienced with my heavenly Father, I realized He was telling me that He would bless me beyond measure for staying on this path even though the pain was tremendous. Emotionally, I waved the white flag of surrender and acknowledged, once again, that God is true to His word.

If He had sent me a handwritten note that day, it might have looked like this:

> *Cindy,*
>
> *I know things are going really great for you and Chris now. It's been a long time coming. I am so happy for you. This baby is hard for you to take right now, I realize. I know that you are in pain. But if you'll trust Me, I will bless you beyond measure for staying on this path. And I promise that one day you'll see this baby as the blessing I created him to be.*
>
> *God*

I experienced a lot of peace that day. Yes, I was still hurting, but the pain I was pushing through also provided me with hope—hope that my God would do what He said He would do. It's a good thing that God had prepared my heart for what was to come.

The Peace That Passes All Understanding

A few months later, in April 2003, Chris received notification from a court in Memphis that he was to appear to settle financial support for Ben. Upon receiving the letter, both our hearts were heavy with this blatant reminder of Chris' sin and the pain his actions had caused. We began taking steps toward dealing with the upcoming change to our lives.

We made the trip to Memphis for the hearing. I was as nervous as could be. Upon entering the courthouse, Chris immediately noticed Michelle. Her mother was sitting with her. We walked toward her, and Chris introduced us. There was absolutely no animosity or negativity in the air, which was a huge relief. We sat down next to them and began to make small talk. It was just a matter of seconds before we started really talking about the reality of our lives. Through tears, I let Michelle know that I hoped to be a wonderful person in Ben's life but that I respected her as his mother. She immediately owned up to her part of the situation and even apologized for causing me pain. I was crying. She was crying. Chris stood by, watching the whole thing in awe.

The hearing went fine and was actually very quick. Afterward, Michelle asked if Chris wanted to see Ben. Chris' eyes lit up, which hurt the deepest part of me. Even though I was praying for a negative DNA test, deep down, I knew that Ben was Chris' son. That feeling was confirmed when Michelle's mom brought Ben up to the courthouse to see Chris. I immediately noticed his chin. He has the Beall chin, just as every other Beall child and grandchild does.

He stared at Chris as if there were no tomorrow. I thought about how precious he was, yet at the same time, I ached inside. My husband shared a child with another woman. I thought to myself, "I'm supposed to be the mother of Chris' children." There was no easy way to explain this situation away. It just hurt.

The court hearing required a paternity test, and God couldn't have timed it any better. Many months earlier, when I was trying to decide whether to stay in the marriage, I told Chris that I didn't want more children with him. I said those exact words to him. Part of me said it to deepen his wound, to let him feel the effect of his actions. The other part of me was just scared to death to have two children to care for if he acted out again. Either way, at that point I was done having kids, and I wanted him to know he would leave this earth with two sons and no more.

However, over the course of a year or better, my heart changed. As I saw my husband's heart not only change but *stay* changed, I decided that maybe another child wasn't such a bad idea. After all, children are a blessing from God, aren't they?

On July 7, 2003, I found out I was expecting another baby. I was elated, as was Chris. And the very next day, the DNA test proved that I was indeed a stepmother to a little boy who was about to have his first birthday. I thought it was awfully sweet of my heavenly Daddy to allow me to hear the joyous news of my pregnancy the day before I found out what I'd been dreading all along. Chris heard the news about the DNA test before I did, and he held me as he told me. I wasn't heartbroken. I'd already adjusted my outlook to include a new little boy in our lives. At that point, I just wanted to know. And in a strange sort of way, I was at peace. Peace came upon just knowing the whole story so we could move forward with the rest of it.

Eight months later, on March 7, 2004, Seth Joseph Beall was born. He was a joy the moment he entered the world. His smile lit up the room, and his red, rosy cheeks always made our hearts flutter. It was almost as if God said, "Hey, here you go. You've done so well this past year. Congratulations." And to think I almost missed him!

The Hard Truth

And of course, there was another adorable, little boy in our lives now.

Sweet little Ben developed a Southern accent and a wonderful charm that wooed us all. Noah absolutely loved him and couldn't wait for his visits. I too enjoyed his presence in our home. I won't say they were always easy and without pain. One of the hardest parts was watching Chris with all three of his boys and knowing that they were all related but I wasn't. A surge of pain penetrated my heart every now and again, but my hope in Christ always trumped the discomfort. And for that I was so grateful.

We have always been up-front with Noah and Seth about their relationship with their brother. We didn't tell them everything at first because we didn't think they could handle it. We often told them, "You'll understand more when you're ten." That answer seemed to suffice for the time being. But once Chris had told Noah about the "birds and the bees," Noah began to wonder more and more about his brother and how he got into this world. One day we had a conversation that took us by surprise.

"Mom...so does Dad have two wives?" Noah asked.

"No, son. I am Dad's only wife."

"Well...then how did Ben get here?" he asked.

"Remember how your dad told you that babies are made?"

"Yes," he said beginning to think to himself. "So...Dad did that with Ben's mom before you were married?"

"No," I told him.

Starting to put two and two together as much as his eight-year-old mind could, he said, "Well, that's not good."

"I know," I said. And then he went about his way.

I called Chris and told him about the situation, and we both knew it was time for Noah to know what happened. When Chris came home, he pulled Noah aside and talked with him about it all. He explained what happened in abbreviated detail because Noah couldn't grasp every part of the story. But Chris did explain that he was sorry for hurting me and sorry that this happened. He told Noah that he wished he hadn't done this, and to that statement Noah cried, "Dad, don't say that because then we wouldn't have Ben!"

One of the most beautiful things about our oldest son is his ability to see the good in situations. He knows that we went through a lot, and he could have blamed an innocent child for making his mom's heart hurt so bad, but he didn't. He loved his brother, and despite the way Ben entered our lives, Noah had no regrets.

No one in our household harbors any animosity, hatred, or anger toward Michelle or anyone in her family. In fact, it's quite the opposite. We all work together to make sure that a little boy knows he is loved. Of course, some days are difficult. There are comments made by a little boy about having an "everyday daddy" that knock me for a loop. There are questions by brothers who wonder why their other brother doesn't have me as a mommy. As these questions come, we answer truthfully and as age-appropriately as possible because the decision to walk in integrity, humility, and God's grace requires this all-out honesty.

I learned a lot from young Noah the day we explained the situation to him. His crystal-clear insight reminded me of what really mattered. I couldn't keep carrying regret and anger because I too couldn't imagine a life without Ben. I learned that God has a big picture and that I play only a small part.

These lessons aren't quickly learned. In fact, you may be wondering how in the world you can go on with life. You might think it's easy for me because my "D-Day" happened more than nine years ago. Well, it's still not easy. The sadness can hit me with such surprising force that I have to remind myself to breathe.

In times like these, you must cling to the Word of God, the encouragement of close friends, and the prayers of those who love you. I know this because that's what I did. I rested in the promises that the Scriptures proclaimed. I spent time with those who were pouring Christ's love into me. I survived solely due to the people who interceded on my behalf. As I did all of this, His peace fell upon me, and even if the peace only lasted a short while, it was worth it. There is no feeling on earth that compares to the peace of the Almighty God of the universe.

Sometimes in life we go through difficult times that don't always makes sense. We question and wonder why we have to endure such things, only to find that our walk through a fiery furnace may provide the only opportunity for someone else to see Jesus.

Maybe your journey through pain will enable others to see Jesus in you and have their eternity forever altered.

Your Healing Journey

1. How have you been able to "go on with life" in the midst of your pain? What helped? What made it harder?

2. Have you ever tried to bargain with God? What was the outcome?

3. Distinguish between the peace of God and the peace the world seeks and talks about. How has your trial helped you turn toward God's peace?

4. Can you think of a time when God brought something good out of something bad that happened? Rest in this remembrance of redemption and let it give you hope during your trial now.

5. Are you willing to endure pain in your life so that your godly response could bring others to Jesus?

A Story of Healing in Their Own Words

MATT AND ANDREA

IT'S BEEN A COUPLE OF YEARS SINCE MATT AND ANDREA first sat on the sofa in our living room. Their fresh wounds and tenderness were apparent by the looks on their faces. But at the same time, something else was present in the midst of their very difficult circumstance: hope.

Matt and Andrea's story is different from the other couples' stories in this book. It wasn't just Matt or just Andrea who was unfaithful. They were both unfaithful, albeit at different times in their marriage. One might think it would be easier to get over infidelity if you did it too. Not so. Read what they have to share.

CINDY: What happened in your life that you never imagined you'd do?

ANDREA: The year Matt was serving in Iraq was the hardest year of my life. Suddenly, hit square in the face with the reality of war, separation, limited communication, and ever-present temptation, our relationship cracked. I searched for comfort, and I found it— in the arms of a man I worked with.

CINDY: Matt, how did you feel when you found out what went on while you were in Iraq?

MATT: While I was there I had suspicions that Andrea was cheating on me. I couldn't prove anything, but I knew something wasn't right with us. When I got home and found out for sure that it had happened, I was devastated.

CINDY: Did you ever think you'd "do such a thing" as commit adultery?

ANDREA: I *never* thought I was the kind of person who would have an affair. I was raised in a strong Christian home and believed firmly in the moral values from my childhood. I loved my husband. I didn't wake up one morning and lose everything I believed in. Satan worked in my heart and mind gradually, feeding me a lie over time. I wasn't capable of having an affair on day one. But after that, I was. I became capable.

MATT: I always told myself, "There's no way I would ever have an affair." I was married, and everything is perfect when you get married, right? I thought that I was in control of my pornography issue and that I could handle it. The thing is, I couldn't handle it. There was no control over this monster I had let into my life.

CINDY: When did you tell Andrea, and what happened next?

MATT: Within a short period of time, I told Andrea everything. The affair, the porn, the lying. We went to church the next day, and I walked into our pastor's office and told him everything. We needed help for the next step. I was cut off from the computer. Andrea locked the computer with a password and installed Covenant Eyes on it to monitor my access. We saw a counselor together. I had to admit to being a porn addict. I had to take something to heart that Chris told me: "Sin cannot live in the light." I had to tell people who I knew would hold me up and keep me accountable for my actions. I had to let go of my pride and let God come into my life and clean me.

CINDY: Andrea, what happened that made you decide to stay?

ANDREA: God never gave me permission to leave, and He gave me every reason to stay. An invaluable friend and mentor to me during the worst days told me that although God allowed divorce in the situation of infidelity (Matthew 5:31-32), He does not always permit you to do so and may ask something different of you.

("'Everything is permissible for me'—but not everything is beneficial" [1 Corinthians 6:12]). He could lead you to stay for just a while, for a little longer, or as in my case, forever. Who knows what God's ultimate plan is and what His reasons are? I can say that by staying I have been a part of something far greater than if I had followed my broken heart.

CINDY: How have you been able to forgive yourself and each other?

ANDREA: Forgiving him was a decision, but it was a decision I did not know how to make until I forgave myself. God gave me an instant moment of forgiveness on a day well into our testimony. In a stream of cleansing tears, I came out forgiven. After that day, I was ready to start truly forgiving Matt. My sin was separated from me in that moment, like oil and water, and that clarity from the Holy Spirit made me able to see my husband the same way.

MATT: Forgiving Andrea was a conscious decision that I actually only made one time. She was my wife, and I didn't want to let that go. I focused on loving Andrea no matter what had happened. That was the moment I made the decision, a conscious thought in my head: "She has made a mistake, but I will let it go and love her anyway."

CINDY: What about trust?

ANDREA: I do struggle with wanting to trust Matt solely when instead I should be relying on God for my true trust, comfort, and peace. It's awkward for me to receive my comfort from God instead of Matt. It seems more logical in this world that Matt could or should prove he is trustworthy, but in all actuality, God is the only one who can give me that trust. Psalm 118:8 says, "It is better to take refuge in the LORD than to trust in man."

MATT: I work daily on being open and transparent with Andrea and those God has placed around me. I'm not always successful at it, but that's the goal. The more transparent I am, the more God's light shines into and out of me. Anything that is hidden leaves room for Satan to move in and attack my marriage, my wife, and me.

CINDY: How is your marriage today?

ANDREA: We are two years into our story. We've had a setback or two. But he's the one I love and adore and the one I want to walk through this with. I made that decision when I chose to forgive. I chose to walk through all of this! Because God asked me to. And I am so blessed that He did. We are the exception, not the rule. I could have missed this.

MATT: Today we know that hard times will come and go, but with each other committed to God and to our marriage, we can weather any storm that comes our way. Our marriage is wonderful. Hard, but wonderful!

7

When Will I Stop Hurting?

GRIEF.

A poignant distress. Deep mental anguish. Acute sorrow. Overwhelming sadness. No wonder we don't want bad things to happen. Um, I'll pass, thank you. Most people associate grief with the death of a person. "He is grieving the loss of his son," or "The grief of losing her mother has devastated her." But grief invades our lives for many different reasons.

"Grief is the normal and natural response to the loss of someone or something important to you. It is a natural part of life. Grief is a typical reaction to death, divorce, job loss, a move away from family and friends, or loss of good health due to illness."[3]

Did you catch that? Grief is more than just experiencing deep sadness and poignant distress because someone close to you has passed away. That may be the most common time people grieve, but I have learned that grief happens anytime there is a loss. The loss of a friendship. The loss of a dream. The loss of innocence. The loss of joy. The loss of expectations. The loss of faithfulness. The loss of anything you held dear.

Let the Crying Begin

Despite the amazing support and love we were shown and the miracles we'd already seen in our marriage, I was still hurting. Some terrific things had occurred in the midst of my suffering, but that didn't mean the images went away. It didn't mean I was completely secure in my marriage. And it certainly didn't mean that trust, admiration, respect, and love were flowing freely from me to my husband. What it did mean is that I put one foot in front of the other, I cried when I needed to cry, and I laughed when laughing was appropriate.

So many people don't deal with their grief adequately. They stuff it down and try to be strong for everyone else, thinking they aren't allowed to feel sadness or they don't have time to step away from routine to truly grieve. But I can tell you with full confidence that even when people are depending on you, even when life has to go on and you must keep moving forward, there has to be time for grieving.

I cried a lot those weeks and months after Chris' confession. I didn't know I had that many tears in me. As I grieved, I healed. My heart started to feel better, and I actually managed to put a smile on my face. I often thought, "Maybe I *can* do this," and I'd suddenly find myself slammed up against a wall with another reality of my current circumstance. So I would grieve some more.

I begged God to help me get through the grief. He was so good to comfort me and to restore my hope as I prayed. Before I knew it, I was going about life again and even enjoying it. I would begin to find my rhythm and to embrace the life I had come to know that included the big A in it, only to be slammed up against said wall *again* within a matter of days because something triggered my crushed heart and made it start bleeding again.

It wasn't until I started down this painful path that I realized that grief comes and goes. It definitely came and went in my life up to this point, but I never really got it. In the early days of a loss, grief is a constant companion, the kind of "friend" who smothers you and gets in your personal space. You give in to that friend, and it gradually starts giving you some room to breathe. But if you don't pay enough attention to it, grief decides it really needs to be close to you again. I grieved the loss of my marriage as I knew it, and as odd as it sounds, I began to heal at the very same time.

One of the things I learned about grief is that you don't lose the person (or the dream or whatever it is you lost) all in one day. You lose him, her, or it gradually as you go about your life. When you experience something that reminds you of what you lost, you grieve. When you see something that takes you back to an old memory, you grieve. That is probably why the first year of a loss is so difficult: the first Christmas, first birthday, first anniversary, first dance recital…many firsts that do not resemble the way things used to be.

When this started happening, I learned that I had to give myself permission to cry, to feel the sadness, to carry the weight of the burden, to realize that if my husband and I made it to a 60-year celebration of marriage, he would not be able to say that he was faithful to me all the days of his life. This was my new life, my new normal. If I didn't do something with all of these emotions, I would never make it through. I had to push through the pain, or it would be with me until I did.

I cried at home, at work, at church, at the grocery store, in front of people, and all by myself. I cried when I felt fear and when I felt joy. I cried when I saw others hurting over my husband's actions, and I cried when I saw him overwhelmed with the mess his actions created. I cried when the tears came on, and I didn't hold them in. If I've learned anything about allowing myself this, it's that if you don't stop the tears when they need to fall, they'll eventually stop themselves.

Physical Loss

Grief is inevitable. At some point we will all experience it whether we like it or not. I have found there to be different types of grief when you lose a person. There is the heart-wrenching grief of losing someone who is very close to you. This grief constantly knocks on your door and can make you beg for death. You think about it whenever you are awake. It's the first thing on your mind when you wake up—that is, assuming the tears stop long enough to allow you to fall asleep. Losing someone close to you will affect your every moment. It will severely rock your world and make you wonder whether you will even be able to breathe again.

Other times you lose people you know, but maybe their presence wasn't in your everyday life. You didn't necessarily see them on a regular basis or even talk to them very often, so this kind of grief doesn't take you completely out of the game. You go about your business, continuing to grocery shop, bathe your kids, go to work, and watch mindless sitcoms, and you don't really give it much thought until someone else says something or your memory is simply triggered. Then you feel a bit sad and maybe even shed a tear, but ultimately, you continue with your normal routine.

Then there are situations where you lose someone who's had a good, long life. Maybe it's your elderly father or great-grandmother who practically raised you. Maybe it's an old Sunday school teacher who impacted your life dramatically. These people have usually watched their grandchildren graduate from high school. Maybe even their great-grandchildren. Some of these people have celebrated 60 years of marriage and buried their own children. They might be in their eighties or nineties. You will experience sadness over their loss, but you are thankful for the great lives they lived on this earth. People around you say, "It was just their time to go."

The Longings Created by Grief

I became well acquainted with grief when I was 18 years old. My dad stood six feet five and weighed 240 pounds. He was a large, imposing man, but in many ways he was the gentlest soul you'd ever meet. And even though I stand close to five feet eleven, I was incredibly intimidated by him.

Two months after my high school graduation, my dad was given the sentence of cancer. Acute myelogenous leukemia, to be exact. My father's body was being overrun by white blood cells.

My dad's eight-month battle with cancer was arduous and diffi-cult for all of us. He went into remission after two months, only to find himself back in a hospital three months after his return home. He seemed so tired, so defeated, so broken. And on March 21, 1990, he took his last breath and was ushered into the presence of Jesus.

I've now lived longer without an earthly father than I did with one. I have forgotten so many things about him and often try to take myself back to the days when he was still with us. But it's hard because what I remember is the smell of the hospital. I remember the room where he stayed, how his bed was positioned, how his large frame gradually became fragile. I remember his hair falling out and when it did, seeing a man who resembled my granddaddy lying in that bed. And I remember the nurses all loving my dad because he was such a charmer even through his misery.

But if I concentrate hard enough, I remember the days on the lake with my dad pulling my brothers and me on water skis. I remember him dancing with my mom in the living room. I remember him sitting in the stands at all of my sporting events and choir concerts.

Even now as I reminisce about my dad, I am grieving. Grieving the dreams and desires that included him. Grieving the fact that he didn't walk me down the aisle. Grieving the fact that he'll never meet my hus-band or my sons. Grieving the fact that he'll never see the college diploma from his alma mater that is proudly displayed on the wall in my study.

Grief isn't enjoyable. How is that for the understatement of the year? We'd all prefer to have our lives all together all of the time. I wouldn't mind it if everyone and everything I loved was always with me and never left. But that's unrealistic. So I accept that grief will come in and out of my life in whatever form it chooses. And you must accept that too. It's a part of life.

"I Know How You Feel"

These types of grief I mentioned are just as applicable, in my opin-ion, when you've lost a dream, a career, or a relationship. They also apply when you've been betrayed and you've lost complete trust in the betrayer.

Sometimes our losses are small, and maybe we are just disappointed that the plans we had in mind for our lives are not coming to pass. Other times a marriage or relationship is so severely tortured and annihilated by callous actions and brutal words that we wonder if our wounded hearts will ever see the light of day, let alone begin to trust again.

I was there.

I don't really like to tell people, "I know how you feel." Even though I very well might have a pretty good idea about how they do feel, I think saying that to someone is an insult. I'm not you. I don't have your demeanor or predicament or past or family history. Even if our circumstances are almost identical, I still don't know how you feel.

But I know how I felt.

I know the deep distress and turmoil that arrived on my doorstep that February morning. I know how it felt to hear the shattering of my future and dreams in an instant. I know how excited, and a little scared, I was about moving to a new city and beginning a new journey in our ministry, only to see it discarded with a few confessional words from my self-absorbed husband. I know the feeling of wondering why I seemed to be so difficult to love by the man I pledged to spend all of my days with. I know *those* feelings because they were my feelings. I know how it felt to realize that my world as I knew it was forever altered, because it was.

Maybe you have felt some of that too. Maybe you wondered why your spouse chose to betray you when all you ever wanted was to grow old together. Maybe you've planned and worked and dreamed about the career path you were sure God would have you take, only to see it fall apart. Maybe you are carrying a heavy burden because the one you want to spend all of your tomorrows with doesn't seem to want to spend his or hers with you, and you have no idea how to love him or her back into your life. Maybe you have no idea how in the world trust and connection can ever be reestablished. And quite frankly, you aren't even sure you want it to. When *that* possibility hits you, the grief can take on yet another dimension. What if you are too broken to *want* to rebuild a life with your spouse?

There are many ways that grief will enter your life. Regardless of the cause, let yourself view it as a part of your healing. There is no way to bypass grief. Oh, we can try. We are so very clever at coming up with new ways to avoid grief, but they are never healthy for us regardless of how long we try them.

If a neighbor, a stranger, a family member, or even your closest friend starts asking you how you are and you become self-conscious about what the right answer is, or if your "free to grieve" card somehow expired before you're ready, don't feel guilty and don't rush yourself past the stages of grief. They do lead to healing and wholeness. The goal is to feel the pain and also to give it to God daily so you can still move forward—even if in teensy, tiny increments—toward a healthy version of you and your new life.

Some folks want you to quickly process the grief because the situation is draining for them or because they need you up and functioning for their own purposes. And it could be that your pain reminds them of their own painful circumstances that they have not yet addressed, and they don't want a living, breathing, sobbing reminder. But most people want to hear that you are doing better because it hurts them to see you sad. Yet sadness just goes with the territory. So do tears.

Encouragement for the Weary

I'd like to offer you a bit of truth, a few nuggets from God's Word that might do your weary soul some good. I don't know about you, but when my heart is heavy or when I am experiencing inconsolable distress, I turn to the only truth I know.

When I found myself camping out in the "how will I live again" train of thought, I clung to the hope that Jesus would do what He said He would do. Did you know that we have a Healer who is fully able and willing to make all things new? "He who was seated on the throne said, 'I am making everything new!' Then he said, 'Write this down, for these words are trustworthy and true'" (Revelation 21:5).

On the days when I wondered how in the world God could make

anything good in my life ever happen again, I trusted His words that He promised to me long ago: "And we know that in all things God works for the good of those who love him, who have been called according to his purpose" (Romans 8:28).

The moments crashed in on me when I wondered how true love and trust would ever be restored, let alone physical intimacy. Then I remembered my Savior's words, "With man this is impossible, but with God all things are possible" (Matthew 19:26).

During the days, minutes, and seconds when I felt utterly alone, I clung to the hope that the Creator of the universe would always be by my side. "Be strong and courageous. Do not be afraid or terrified because of them, for the LORD your God goes with you; he will never leave you nor forsake you" (Deuteronomy 31:6).

And in the years after the dreadful confession that sent my world spiraling downward, I rested in the truth that God would not only bind up my very battered heart but also bring me freedom like I've never tasted, lavish upon me a beautiful future from the demolished ruins that once were my marriage, and finally return to me years upon years of blessing because I trusted in His promises.

> The Spirit of the Sovereign LORD is on me, because the LORD has anointed me to preach good news to the poor. He has sent me to bind up the brokenhearted, to proclaim freedom for the captives and release from darkness for the prisoners, to proclaim the year of the LORD's favor and the day of vengeance of our God, to comfort all who mourn, and provide for those who grieve in Zion—to bestow on them a crown of beauty instead of ashes, the oil of gladness instead of mourning, and a garment of praise instead of a spirit of despair. They will be called oaks of righteousness, a planting of the LORD for the display of his splendor. They will rebuild the ancient ruins and restore the places long devastated; they will renew the ruined cities that have been devastated for generations (Isaiah 61:1-4).

I took God at His Word. You can too.

I wish I could tell you that whatever you've lost will be returned to you. That if you've lost all hope in your marriage, you will one day be in a hope-filled marriage that is full of mutual respect, honor, and submission. That if you've got a particular dream in life, you should pursue it, and it will come to pass. But I can't. I don't know the mysteries of God. I don't know which marriages will be saved, which bodies will be healed, or which dreams will be accomplished on this earth. But I do know that He will carry you while you grieve your loss. I can't promise you that God will restore to you what's been lost, but please know He will restore you.

Growing Pains

If you allow yourself to look back on your past experiences, I think you will find that the times when you hurt the most were the times when you grew the most. There is something about going through pain that brings about change. There are those who choose to allow the pain to sink them, but you are not going to be one of them. I just know it.

So many of us hate going through the pain. We fight it and often try to ignore it. No one really enjoys enduring the pain of going through a fire, but if we are all honest with ourselves, we'll admit that we like the results of the fire. If instead of fighting and ignoring the pain, we will embrace it, we will find our Savior just waiting with comfortable, open arms to carry us through it. And we'll be blown away at the changes in our lives because of it.

If you are suffering pain right now like you've never known, rest assured that it won't last forever. If you are not going through pain right now, you eventually will. So regardless of where you are in life, pain will be a part of it. I'm not trying to "speak" anything over you by any means. I am simply stating what the Bible says: "For our light and momentary troubles are achieving for us an eternal glory that far outweighs them all" (2 Corinthians 4:17).

It would take pages to list the Scriptures that address trouble in our lives. So many of them encourage us to stay strong and not fret when we face troubles. In my finite mind, I can only conclude that we will endure them. We can't just skip out on a season of trial. We have to graduate from it.

Compared to what awaits us as Christ followers one day, our pain in life is small even when it feels paralyzing. Please hear me...your pain is valid. And it's okay to hurt. In fact, feeling the pain and grieving your situation is absolutely necessary in order to see the growth one day. But I don't want you to live there, because there is hope. And that hope comes through faith in God's outstanding power to bring healing. I'm living proof.

Nothing is too difficult for Him.

Your Healing Journey

1. Have you lost someone close to you? If so, write down in your journal or discuss with your group how you felt when it happened.

2. Do you deal with your grief in a healthy way, or do you push it aside and hope it will go away on its own? What can you do today to help yourself make the shift toward healthy grieving so you can reach healing as God intends for you?

3. What other losses have you experienced in your life? How did you feel when these losses left a void? What adjectives could you use to describe your mental, physical, emotional, and spiritual state during that time?

4. Whom do you turn to when immense sadness and grief have bombarded your life? If your spouse is the one who triggered your grief, whom (outside of the relationship) should you turn to for the healthy, godly advice and guidance you need? Mom

5. What are some of the profound lessons you've learned about life, others, or yourself through your hardships?

8

How Can I Learn to Trust and Forgive?

MUSIC WAS MY FIRST PASSION. My mom says I used to lie in my bed as a toddler and sing my heart out. As I grew, so did my love for music. I sang in choirs at church, in high school, and again in college. I could read music fairly well thanks to six years of piano lessons. And although I didn't have a fabulous voice, I had a good ear and could pick out just about any harmony in any song. When I was singing or playing music, I felt like myself. I felt close to God and at home in my own life.

When Chris confessed everything to me, we had been leading worship together for many years. My life was filled with music, and so were our entire nine years of marriage. On the day he "came clean" and the walls of my family and marriage came tumbling down, my cherished tie to worship music was broken as well.

Right away, I was faced with my first lesson in learning to trust. I needed to completely trust God with every part of my life—the losses, the pain, and the next steps. Our journey to trust and forgive people who have betrayed us begins with trusting God.

When God Gives a Passion

My friend Dea says, "When God displaces, He replaces." And sure enough, a desire and hunger to write grew into a new passion for me. I love writing so much that at any moment in the day I am probably constructing sentences in my mind. When I have any downtime or am driving long distances, I start writing in my mind. When insomnia hits, it's not uncommon for me to get out of bed, grab my laptop, and start writing. God replaced the joy of my music passion with a new passion that lets me communicate my soul and my being. Just like singing, writing centers me, and it allows me to express my heart in ways that my vocal cords couldn't even do. It was the perfect replacement. God's good at that!

God did that for me, and He will do it for you. If you have lost a passion because of an ongoing trial or struggle in your marriage or some other change you didn't see coming, know that the Creator of your heart can place new desires there. — *Teaching piano*

Rebuilding Trust in People

I am thrilled to be able to express myself by writing on my personal blog. It gives me creative license to perfect my gift, and it is also a tool to help other women who've walked down the same road of infidelity that I have walked. Many people just aren't as far along on their journey as I am.

Every week I receive e-mails from women who ask many questions about getting through infidelity in their marriage. Of all the questions I am asked, one of the most common is, "How did you learn to trust him again?" And every time I give the same answer: I am still learning.

I would love to be able to come up with the perfect algebraic formula that shows exactly how to restore trust. But that isn't going to happen—not because I barely squeezed out of algebra with a 71 percent, but because trust and forgiveness don't exist in the land of numbers. They are born of God's grace, mercy, and healing.

It would be really nice if I could paint the most amazing piece of artwork to show you the mystical, beautiful way that forgiveness blossoms from a hardened heart. But I can only draw stick figures. Besides, the only drawing we are asked to do is to draw our strength and our hope from God's grace. This is true for every trial, every heartbreak, and every betrayal we experience.

I am still on my journey of having my trust restored in my husband, but I have learned a few things that I hope you will find helpful. And remember, you don't have to have endured infidelity in your marriage to lose trust. Trust can be broken in many different ways.

I believe that the enemy of my soul wants my marriage to tumble into the abyss. He has made many attempts to destroy us, but they didn't work. We have been badly bruised and have lots of scars from the war, but we were not taken down. And I think that ticks him off. In fact, I know it does. Which is why, I believe, he is coming back after me in a mental battle. If he can't get our marriage to fail and end in divorce, and if he can't turn us against God, he is going to do everything in his power to make me feel as if all our healing and hope will one day run out.

How will I know if he succeeds? How will you know if he succeeds in your life? The day we live in fear and allow our minds and hearts to worry about situations that may never occur is a day he is winning. These moments of fret and hopelessness are a complete waste of my precious time and my precious life and marriage. The same is true for your life, my friend. We are experiencing restoration, and we needn't look beyond God for our truth and courage.

The Restoration of Integrity

My husband is an amazing man. Are you a little bit shocked that I can say that with complete honesty and sincerity? That, my friend, is redemption—when I can see and state the truth even in the chaos and pain.

From the moment of Chris' confession, his goal has been to restore my trust in him. Even when I doubt and question him, he does not get defensive or have a "get over it" attitude. He knows his actions caused me indescribable pain, and he accepts the responsibility as his own. He will do anything to help me feel secure in our marriage. He has laid down his life for me.

One evening, Chris had to work late. He was overseeing something at work, and his team had to spend several hours getting things completed. He rarely works late, so this was not a big deal for me. He, on the other hand, wanted to make sure I wasn't worrying or letting my mind take a journey down a fretful road.

Around 8:00 that evening, Chris called me to let me know how the progress was going. After we chatted a bit, he said, "Hey, why don't you talk to John for a few minutes, okay?" John picked up the phone and said, "Hey Cindy! How's it going?" I answered him, and we made some small talk. Toward the end of the conversation he said, "I just wanted to let you know we've been working hard tonight and we'll make him get out of here in a couple of hours."

That is how trust is restored. Humility, honor, and consistent assurance—even when providing that assurance is difficult, inconvenient, and uncomfortable.

As you know, our entire LifeChurch.tv congregation and staff know about our story. Most people see it as a miracle and also know we are still in progress. (Aren't we all?) So when Chris Beall hands his friends the phone and says, "Why don't you talk to Cindy," they know what it's about. And when I hear him say, "Why don't you talk to John, okay?" I know what it's about. It's about a husband who wants to ensure that his wife's heart is safe, so he humbles himself and asks for help along the way.

Honor and Humility Grow Trust

My husband absolutely loves his job, but he loves his family more. And because of that, I have been blessed to watch honesty and integrity grow in his life. In his previous role at LifeChurch.tv, he had to do some traveling. Not every week, but every couple of months he had to visit the campuses he used to lead. When he traveled, someone almost always went with him. Sometimes it was a coworker, and other times it was one of our sons. However, when it didn't work out for someone to go with him, he'd stay in the home of a staff member. His humility shows through because sometimes that staff member is someone who reports to him in the work setting. He lets go of pride and lets that person know that this is now part of his life and part of his restoration.

Many men or women might not be willing to do such a thing because of pride, ego, or just plain shyness. It takes great courage to ask someone to be a part of your healing path. I am so thankful that Chris takes the high road, owns his actions, accepts responsibility, and walks in humility. Is anything more attractive? I think not.

Trust Means Taking a Risk

It breaks my heart to know that some people think they can just pick up where they left off. My husband works hard, but I still struggle. I wish I could say otherwise, but I'd be lying.

Isn't that the way it is with all of us? I've come to realize that we are all capable of doing things we never imagined we'd do. So trusting a person is a risk. We must learn to trust people, but we must also realize that people will fail us. It's part of life. But if we place our utmost trust in our heavenly Daddy, we will never be let down.

I mentioned earlier that a mental battle is going on inside me as I strive to trust my husband more every day. I engage in this battle on a regular basis, and it can be exhausting. But the more I do it and believe what God has shown me, the easier it becomes.

When this battle begins, I stand on the one thing that is trustworthy and never fails. I stand on the Word of God. Praise Him that His words are sharper than any double-edged sword (Hebrews 4:12). There is power in them, and when we claim them, believe in them, stand on them, and trust in them, we will be lifted up. We will find peace.

The Bible says in Proverbs 3:5-6, "Trust in the LORD with all your heart and lean not on your own understanding; in all your ways acknowledge him, and he will make your paths straight." The Hebrew word for *trust* is *batach*. It means to have confidence. And do you know how *Webster's* defines the word *confidence*? "Faith or belief that one will act in a right, proper, or effective way." So for us to *batach* in the Lord means that we have to have faith that God will act in a right, proper and effective way. (Which He most certainly will, by the way.)

When the struggle comes, instead of entertaining thoughts that I believe are straight from the enemy, I remind myself of what God's Word says. I have found a few passages that give me courage to face the scary path that lies ahead of me. When I quote them aloud, the enemy flees.

> Surely God is my salvation; I will trust and not be afraid. The LORD, the LORD, is my strength and my song; he has become my salvation (Isaiah 12:2).

> Blessed is the man who trusts in the LORD, whose confidence is in him (Jeremiah 17:7).

> We demolish arguments and every pretension that sets itself up against the knowledge of God, and we take captive every thought to make it obedient to Christ (2 Corinthians 10:5).

> You, dear children, are from God and have overcome them, because the one who is in you is greater than the one who is in the world (1 John 4:4).

> In all these things we are more than conquerors through him who loved us. For I am convinced that neither death nor life, neither angels nor demons, neither the present nor the future, nor any powers, neither height nor depth, nor anything else in all creation, will be able to separate us from the love of God that is in Christ Jesus our Lord (Romans 8:37-39).

> Be merciful to me, O God, for men hotly pursue me; all day long they press their attack. My slanderers pursue me all day long; many are attacking me in their pride. When I

am afraid, I will trust in you. In God, whose word I praise,
in God I trust; I will not be afraid. What can mortal man
do to me? (Psalm 56:1-4).

Look again at that last verse. David freely admits that he is afraid.
And rightly so! But then he reminds himself just how trustworthy his
God is. One minute he's afraid and chooses to trust in God. The very
next minute he declares he will not be afraid because he trusts in God.

I often find myself sounding a lot like King David did here. One
moment I make statements based on my feelings of fear, and the next
moment I remember the truth and decide to stand on it. The same
thing may happen the next day—and the day after that. I have learned
that if I speak God's truth over my heart enough, it eventually sinks in.
It gets into the blood that courses through my veins.

When people go through situations that rock their worlds, that
destroy their trust and even their hope in mankind, they want to fix
whatever is broken—fast. Unfortunately, trust isn't a destination we
reach; it's a path we walk. Every single day.

The bottom line for me is that when Chris is walking in the fruit
of God's Spirit, I can fully trust him. But it's not really Chris I trust—
I trust Jesus in him.

Trust in Jesus.

Replace Anger with Forgiveness

"I'll never forgive you."

You've probably heard someone say these words before. And you
realize that's a death sentence, right? You may have said those words
with the intent to inflict pain on the recipient, but saying those words
will cause you to endure a slow, bitter, decimation of the soul that will
eventually eat away at you from the inside out. It's not a pleasant phrase
to hear when you are guilty of causing pain to another. It's certainly not
good to be the one saying it.

A shallow and immature action can cause you to forfeit the trust of someone you love dearly. Restoring trust is important. But so is learning to forgive.

We've all been wounded. I am no stranger to the pain I see in the eyes of so many people. We can try to cover it up and "get over it," but if we don't truly forgive, we will be stunted individuals going about our lives and becoming more and more embittered. Forgiveness is essential. It's also possible.

My dad was a little hotheaded. He often got frustrated about the smallest things and took his wrath out on my brothers and me. I regularly walked on eggshells, wondering when his German blood would start to boil. My goal was often to just make it through the day without making my dad angry. He never laid a hand on me, but his words and discouraging looks often cut my heart into a million pieces. It would have been ridiculous of me to expect apologies because they just never came. So I had to learn how to deal with my anger, frustration, and near hatred for the man I called my dad. I could no longer hang on to the grudge that had grown in my heart, or it would make me an incredibly bitter young woman.

The Legacy of Forgiveness

Having to forgive didn't start in our generation. God's Word contains stories of betrayal that call for forgiveness by those who have been wounded. Take Jacob, for instance. We learn in Genesis 29 that he had eyes for the younger daughter of Laban, who was named Rachel. He made a deal with her father to work for him for seven years so he could marry her. The time came, but Laban tricked Jacob into marrying the older daughter, Leah. Jacob didn't realize what happened until the next morning.

Clearly Jacob was betrayed by Laban even though the custom was that the older daughter would marry before the younger daughter. Laban knew the custom, yet he promised Jacob the hand of his younger daughter, Rachel. I imagine Jacob had to figure out how to forgive his father-in-law.

One of the worst stories of betrayal was that of Joseph and his brothers, recorded in Genesis 37. The baby boy of the family got himself into some sticky situations. Wearing the colorful robe that your daddy gave you and parading around in front of your brothers is probably not the best idea. But he did it anyway. Not only that, but telling them about your dream of them bowing down to you one day? Bad idea, Joseph. His actions landed him far away from his family. The story doesn't end terribly, but I imagine that while Joseph trudged along as a slave or sat in an Egyptian dungeon, he had to work through forgiving his brothers for robbing him of his very life.

The Bible doesn't mince words when it comes to forgiveness. We don't have to wonder what our heavenly Father thinks about the idea. He's the author of forgiveness, and we'd do well to follow His commands about the subject. Matthew 6:14-15 says, "If you forgive other people when they sin against you, your Father in heaven will also forgive you. But if you do not forgive others their sins, your Father will not forgive your sins."

The Greek word for *forgive* in this verse is *aphiemi*, which means in the simplest definition, "to send away." If we took the verses above and put the definition in place of the word *forgive*, it might read something like this: "If you send away the sins of others, your Father in heaven will also send away your sins. But if you don't send away the sins of others, your Father in heaven will not send away your sins."

Ouch. That stings a bit, doesn't it? Especially when you've been wounded so badly by someone you've loved as unconditionally as possible. It sounds like a cruel joke to expect us to just let it go, doesn't it?

Colossians 3:13 says, "Bear with each other and forgive whatever grievances you may have against one another. Forgive as the Lord forgave you." If you know Jesus as your Lord and Savior, you know that you have a sinful nature. If we don't recognize that nature, we won't recognize our need for a Savior. We also need to understand and remember the true meaning of God's love. "While we were still sinners, Christ died for us" (Romans 5:8). If we truly understand God's forgiveness, can we really withhold our forgiveness from those who have hurt us?

Stop Nursing Your Wounds

It can become second nature to tend to our wounds with such care that we begin to identify only with the wound and not with a life of healing or restoration. When something reminds us of our pain, we nurse the hurt and then just can't get past it. It's almost as if we forget that we, too, need a Savior. We're so busy saying, "Look at my hurt!" that we forget to give it over to God.

Romans 3:23 says, "All have sinned and fall short of the glory of God." The last time I checked, *all* really did mean *all*. Which includes you and me. Sure, I haven't been unfaithful to my husband physically, but I have committed sins too. And when we sin, we are not just sinning against one person; we are also sinning against our heavenly Father.

You see, the key to learning true forgiveness is this: No more comparing. We have to quit comparing our sins to the sins of others because the standard will always change. Instead of looking at our sin in light of Christ's perfection, we start looking at the people around us. "Well, I'm not as bad as Sam. Do you know the things he's done?"

When we compare our sin with the sins of others, we turn our standard into a moving target. That means we will never have a consistent benchmark. Our standard for measuring up should never be horizontal. It should be vertical. We should do exactly what the book of Hebrews says and "fix our eyes on Jesus, the author and perfecter of our faith" (Hebrews 12:2). When we do that, we realize just how short we fall.

I know how hard this is. I am profoundly aware of how badly my flesh wants to throw my husband's sin back in his face when he gets mad at me for something small. I know how easily I could remind him of his failures and make sure he knows just how picture-perfect *my* marital résumé is. But reacting like that will never bring about forgiveness.

I don't have to remind you that Christ lived a perfect, sinless life on this earth. He did nothing wrong. Ever. And when I find that I am struggling with forgiving someone, it's usually because I get into the "I can't believe she did such a thing" mind-set and shift my focus from Jesus to the person who just, for lack of better words, fell short. I find that when I keep my focus on Christ and strive to walk with Him daily, I almost always walk in forgiveness toward others and gratitude for what Christ did for me.

Don't Wait Until You Feel Like Forgiving

One of the harder parts of forgiveness is that we don't always feel like forgiving. The problem is that feelings are often misleading and erratic. So to rely on the unreliable for something as transforming as forgiveness is to miss out on a chance to heal and move forward.

I learned a long time ago that you rarely feel your way into positive actions, but you can act your way into better feelings. You may not really want to wake up at five for that morning run, but you do it anyway. Afterward, you are so glad you made the extra effort because you feel good and have more energy. There is great satisfaction in making a choice to do something that your flesh was yelling at you not to do! You acted your way into a feeling.

My pastor says, "We judge others by their actions, but we judge ourselves by our intentions." He couldn't be more right. When I do something to hurt others, I rarely mean to do it. I mean, I'm not a cruel person, and I genuinely try to encourage people and not hurt them. So when I do hurt others' feelings, I am easier on myself and don't get too mad at me. But when others hurt me, I assume they are out to destroy me. That they want to make my life miserable. Chances are, they are not, and they just made a mistake—just as I do on a daily basis. Why don't I give them the benefit of the doubt the way I do for myself?

How to Know You're Healing

The results of forgiveness look different for everyone. Some relationships will be mended in spite of betrayal, and some will end because of it. The key, though, is to make sure you are healing from this wound. You don't want to get a knot in your stomach every time you think about this person, especially if he or she is your spouse. Here's one way you can know you have healed from a wound caused by someone else: You cease to feel resentment against your offender. My mentor says, "You know you've healed from the hurt that someone else's actions have caused when you can look back on the situation and it's just a fact."

We all make mistakes. We all have done things we regret. We all need forgiveness. And we all need to extend that same forgiveness to others—not just today, but every day.

It's time to forgive.

Your Healing Journey

1. Cindy shares that she grieved the loss of music in her life after Chris' confession. Is there anything outside your marriage that you've lost and had to grieve? Has a replacement risen up in your life yet?

   Giving up teaching...

2. Does rebuilding trust seem like an impossibility to you? What are your current obstacles to trusting another person?

3. Do you feel that your spouse is willing to restore your trust? How does that make you feel? If he or she isn't willing, what steps can you take as a couple to unite and work toward mutual trust?

yes ... hopeful

4. Do you trust God a lot, a little, or not at all? Why or why not?

5. Do you struggle with forgiving people when they wound you? If so, why do you think you struggle?

6. When have you compared your sins to another person's sin? Why did you feel compelled to do that? What was the result?

7. If people don't apologize or act sorry for hurting you, how can you forgive them? What steps do you need to take today to extend forgiveness?

A Story of Healing in Their Own Words

WADE AND CHRISTI

EACH OF THE STORIES I'VE SHARED WITH YOU has a special place in my heart. I have watched some of them unfold right before my very eyes and have learned about others after the fact. This story is extra special to me because I was privy to almost every bit of it from the beginning to where it is today. You'll soon see why it touches me so deeply.

It was mid-June 2008, when my dear friend Jessica called me. She was beside herself because she recently learned of her brother's infidelity in his marriage. When she heard the news, she immediately thought of Chris and me and felt that maybe we could help since...well, you know, we've been there, done that.

She asked if I would consider talking to her mother. I spent a good hour on the phone with Jessica's mother, Margie, because she was obviously distressed about what was going on in her baby boy's marriage. I tried to encourage her as best as I could, but the situation was looking bleak because her daughter-in-law, Christi, was ready to throw in the towel and call it quits. And rightly so. I felt the same thing after learning about Chris' infidelity. It's a natural, understandable response to such horrid news.

Jessica, Margie, and I joined forces and began to pray for reconciliation. I specifically prayed that if God wanted me to speak with Christi, He would have her contact me. She had heard of my story through Jessica and knew what Chris and I had been through. She had not contacted me in the weeks that followed her husband's confession, so I could only assume she was not interested in hearing what I had to say. So I kept praying. Fast-forward six weeks.

Christi bought a one-way ticket from her home in Florida to visit her family in Texas. She wasn't entirely sure she would be returning to Wade. However, in the midst of her desire to remove herself from her marriage, she decided to go to a Beth Moore simulcast at a church about 45 minutes from where she was staying.

She attended the Friday evening session and was moved to tears. Noticing that Christi was sitting alone and fully emotional, another lady, Joyce, approached her. Christi shared with this stranger all that she was going through, and Joyce said, "Please come back tomorrow morning. I want you to meet someone."

Saturday morning dawned, and Christi awoke with a sense of anticipation. She traveled back to the church where she met with God the night before. When she arrived, she found Joyce standing with a group of ladies. Noticing her, Joyce pulled her friend Nancy aside and walked toward Christi.

After polite introductions, Christi began to share her story with Nancy. After a short amount of time, Nancy said, "My daughter went through a similar experience. She lives in Oklahoma, but I know she'd love to talk to you." And then Nancy, my mother, took out her phone, and Christi called me. (This is the part where you place your hand under your jaw and push your mouth closed.)

Now, I am a firm believer in the fact that the God I love, know, and serve is the God of the impossible. There is nothing too difficult for him. I believe it. I've preached it. I've lived it. But to say that I was utterly astounded would be a gross understatement. I mean, of all of the churches in Texas (and there are a lot), she chose to go to the one where my mother, of all people, would be. I mean, for the love of Peter, Paul, and Mary! Does it get any clearer than that?

Christi journeyed four states away from her problems, only to find that God would chase her down wherever she went. After talking with me for half an hour, she asked if she and her husband could come see us. So after Wade made his way to Texas, they drove six hours north to

Oklahoma. We spent five hours together that night. Our eyelids were heavy, but our hearts were full. Even though Christi was still upset and Wade was still walking in a thick cloud of shame, there was hope in their eyes. And in their hearts. Here's the journey that they've been on for the past couple of years.

❧

CINDY: What was your initial response when you found out about Wade's infidelity?

CHRISTI: I was hurt, angry, devastated, humiliated, and depressed. The anger was the most confusing for me because I've never been an angry person. I'd never really wanted to hit someone or scream at anyone, but this was different.

CINDY: Wade, did you ever think you'd "do such a thing" as commit adultery?

WADE: Never! I was raised in a solid, Christian home. I began my relationship with Jesus Christ at a very young age. I was a virgin when I got married. But my ugly habit of pornography took ahold and had a very negative effect on my life. Even as I look back at when I was cheating, it still feels very surreal. I still can't believe I was that deep in sin.

CINDY: Christi, what happened that made you decide to stay?

CHRISTI: God had been trying to get my attention for several weeks, and I had done everything I could to ignore Him. But when I sat in that church in Texas with your mother, I could not deny that God wanted something different for my life. That day I was able to tell my husband that I wanted to try to make it work.

CINDY: How have you been able to forgive Wade?

CHRISTI: There were a lot of things in my life that I needed to work on—codependency, past hurts, self-esteem issues, and some unforgiveness. When I decided to work on myself and let God have control of my husband, I was able to start forgiving him. It was definitely not instant! It was a very long and hard process.

CINDY: Wade, do you ever find yourself walking in shame because of what you did? What does living in brokenness mean for you?

WADE: This has been one of the hardest parts of recovery for me. My past really hurts me. I'd give almost anything to get it all back. I'm happy with the way God has intervened in my life and saved my marriage, but I still hate that I betrayed my wife, my Lord, my parents, and everyone else in my life.

CINDY: What about trust?

CHRISTI: A wise woman (that's you, Cindy) once told me that I would not be able to trust my husband, but that I could trust God in my husband. That is exactly what I am doing. I see Wade striving to follow God and lead our family in God's will, and that makes it easier to trust him.

WADE: This is an ongoing battle. I believe that every day that goes by with me being faithful to my wife is another day that she regains a little bit of trust. My guess is that she'll always have a little bit of doubt about my actions for the rest of our lives. I recognize it is my responsibility to go the extra mile to make sure I show her transparency and honesty.

CINDY: When you look at Christi now, how does it make you feel?

WADE: I look at Christi differently today than I ever did. When someone shows another person the grace she has shown me, it's impossible not to! Christi is more beautiful to me now than she was the day I met her. We experience intimacy at levels we never experienced before. And that was something I wasn't sure we would ever have!

CINDY: How is your marriage today?

CHRISTI: Headed in the right direction. We have come a long way, and so many parts of our marriage are better than they have ever been. I know we still need to work on some things, but we are committed to doing that together.

WADE: It's a work in progress. I wish I could write that we are totally healed and our marriage is now perfect, but I can't. We still argue, my past still haunts us (albeit not as much), I still get on her nerves with my odd sense of humor, and we still get short with each other, but we have a new foundation to build on. We also have a truly amazing miracle to look back on that reminds us that God really loves us!

9

Leaning on the Strength of Others

WHEN WE GO THROUGH SOMETHING HEART WRENCHING, let alone humiliating, it's natural to want to isolate ourselves from the world and even from those closest to us. With determination and a bit of stubbornness, we go about our lives trying to put the pain behind us, to suffer in silence. Pride might hold us back, but sometimes it is just plain difficult to know how to reach out to others when we are broken. It is hard to muster the energy to relay our troubles to other people and to seek out those worthy of our confidence and confession.

However hard it is to talk about your concerns or issues, you do need the strength, wisdom, and guidance of godly people for what you are going through right now and for all that you will face as you keep working on the particular areas of need and healing.

Chris and I learned early on that sitting around our dining table staring at each other was not going to help. In fact, that self-assigned isolation put undue pressure on both of us when we had enough worries and fears circling around our heads.

Seeking Support

We first came to LifeChurch.tv in September 2001. Chris was apply-ing for a worship pastor position, and we came in for the weekend to lead worship. We met Jim and Beth that weekend and were immedi-ately drawn to them. We found out later that they felt the exact same way about us. Call it kindred spirits or divine flow; it was something driven by God's Spirit, and we could not explain it. We later learned why God placed that in all of us. The road we would eventually walk together would be rocky.

Chris' confession rocked our entire church staff. He had only been there six weeks when he confessed his addiction and infidelity. Amaz-ingly, all accepted him right away. People were so excited when Chris joined the team and equally saddened that he had fallen. I'm sure there were moments of judgment on their part, which is understandable. But for the most part, there was love and encouragement for him.

Jim was also a pastor on the church staff, which was relatively small compared to what it is now. Jim and Chris didn't spend a great deal of time together, but the size of the staff allowed them to at least begin a friendship, which would prove to be vital in the process of restoring our marriage.

Although Chris moved to Oklahoma in early January 2002, I stayed behind until our home sold. By February 7, I was in Edmond, ready to begin a new season in our life. On February 18, my doorbell rang. Upon answering it, I found Beth holding a bouquet of flowers. I invited her in, and our relationship was set for life. Little did I know how soon I'd need her friendship.

The very next day was the day everything changed. Without a friend in sight, I immediately thought of Beth, but I had no intentions of call-ing her. I had always been the one people came to for advice and help. My pride was hijacking my sense of reality because I really needed her but didn't want to reach out. A day later, Chris and I found out that Jim and Beth were going to meet with us. Having no idea what the meeting was about, we gladly agreed. If they could help us shoulder this burden at all, we were game.

The day after Chris' confession, "Miss Beth," as many affectionately call her, pulled up in my driveway to whisk me away for a visit. Clearly my face was distraught. I've never been one to hide my true feelings. Faking my way through something never happens. You get what you see with me. And Miss Beth got a lot that night.

We pulled into the Sonic drive-in to order a drink. She willingly pulled out her wallet and pushed my hand aside when I reached for mine. It was as if she knew that money would be scarce for us, so she didn't expect me to pay.

There wasn't much small talk between us. We dove right in and began hashing out all that had transpired during the past 36 hours. In her encouraging way, she attempted to downplay the situation so that my tears could take a break. My cheeks had become their temporary home over the last day and a half, and I was plumb worn out. Unfortunately, I'd soon learn that this day would be replayed over and over again—kind of like my own *Groundhog Day*, but Bill Murray didn't play the leading role. I did.

If you asked me to tell you what Miss Beth said to me that night while we were sipping our sodas in the parking lot, I couldn't. I don't remember if she gave great advice. I don't remember if she told a joke. I don't remember if I had an "aha moment" with her. What I do remember is that she was there. And that was what I needed.

You Aren't Alone

When hard times hit, so many of us think we're the only ones who've endured such difficult situations. The reality is that all people have endured some type of difficulty in their lives. That's just how life works. Pain and trouble and conflict will be involved. Many couples have not walked through an adulterous situation, but they have walked through something else just as devastating.

Jim and Beth had not always been in full-time ministry. They spent the better part of their lives contributing to a family business. Early on, they faced something that too many couples in America face in their marriage covenant. They too had experience with infidelity.

Sound familiar? Earlier in this chapter I told you that we felt a connection with Jim and Beth from the beginning, but we just could not put a finger on it. Well, we put our finger on it. They had endured infidelity and survived. They have actually done better than just survive; they have flourished and grown as a couple.

It was only appropriate that they were "assigned" to us. They had endured the same trial, and their children were now grown, which gave them the freedom to spend large amounts of time with us. And boy did they ever.

The frequency of their visits to our home was astounding. They were literally at our beck and call. Not because we demanded them to be, but because they knew we needed them. We communicated with them every day, and they typically knew when we needed a visit. They didn't wait for us to ask. They knew the emotional damage we were trying to repair and wanted to be available at any time.

When I was in Texas visiting my family I was afraid to leave Chris alone because I wasn't sure if he'd cheat on me again. I hoped that he learned his lesson, but at that time, I didn't trust him farther than I could throw him. And friends, that was not very far.

In order to soothe my wounded heart and help me feel a little more secure, Jim decided to come by our house every night to check on Chris while I was gone. When he did, he asked him for his car keys. Chris willingly handed them over to Jim. And every morning, Jim brought the keys back to Chris. Jim did this for ten days in a row. Most people wait a lifetime to have a friend like Jim. Both he and Beth went above and beyond the call of duty to minister to us.

We definitely did not want Jim and Beth to endure adultery in their marriage, but God used their experience to help us.

For me, Beth was such a tremendous source of encouragement that I began to believe that life after adultery was possible. And not just an ordinary life, but an extraordinary one filled with God's love and forgiveness! I didn't cause the scandalous situation in my marriage, but Beth was quick to help me focus on me and how I could change and grow as a believer in Christ through this. It would have been so easy for me to point my finger at Chris and keep it on him, but she would not let me get away with that. Beth repeatedly challenged me in one moment and then followed it up with a hug and great big smile in the next. She was forcefully gentle.

Jim was also walking Chris through a myriad of issues, including rebuilding my trust in him. Jim was very much a positive influence in Chris' life, but he also let Chris know that the road he chose was going to be very much an uphill climb, at least for a few years. Chris embraced that, took responsibility for his actions, and worked his tail off to win back my trust. Had it not been for Jim's and Beth's direct mentoring in our marriage, I feel quite certain we would not have made it.

Expanding the Circle

You don't have to set up a chat room and invite strangers to discuss your personal life, but it is very beneficial to have a support network that extends beyond a couple of family or church members. For one thing, it can be a lot of responsibility for just one or two people to be mentoring or shepherding you and your spouse through your difficulty. Not only did Jim and Beth play a huge role in our lives, but so did the small group we were a part of. I remember walking into the first evening meeting. I was so nervous. I didn't really want to be there because I felt so vulnerable. I would rather have just stayed home, but I'm certain my being "persuaded" to be there was a God thing. It's not the most comfortable thing walking into a group of people you consider strangers. Fortunately for us, they didn't see us in the same light. It was like they knew us.

Again, I can't remember many things that happened that night, but I do remember one thing. During our sharing, a woman named Elizabeth came over to us, plopped herself right in front of us, grabbed our hands, and told us in a roundabout way that we were going to live through this. I wasn't used to that sort of encounter, someone telling me what the future held. But for some reason, I listened and believed everything she said. Chris and I were both crying with the group look-ing on. As Billy and Rhonda led us in music, we cried even more. I've been told that "tears cleanse the windows of the soul." I think my win-dows were spotless that night.

This group loved us, prayed for us, invited us to their homes, and held our hands as we cried. I know Jesus was proud as He watched His kids do what He'd been commanding them to do for centuries.

We had tremendous support from many believers in Christ, but there were some who thought I should walk away from the marriage. When I chose to stay, we lost a few relationships. I guess they just couldn't survive the aftermath of Chris' actions. It hurt us deeply that this happened, but we know that sometimes that is part of the deal.

Honor in Honesty

I cannot write this chapter without mentioning our senior pastor, Craig Groeschel, and his leadership role. To say Chris' confession was difficult for him is putting it mildly. This situation had the makings of a very controversial story. He could have just removed Chris and said that we'd had a "change of heart," but Craig believed that telling the truth was the only route to take.

Craig was taken aback by the information. He could have thrown Chris under the bus and let him fend for himself. Sadly enough, many church leaders have done just that to their own.

Not Craig.

He took the high road, just as he usually does. Despite the fresh wound to his heart and betrayal that Chris' addiction and infidelity caused, he chose to bring hope and help to a very broken man and his family. Either he or his wife, Amy, called me weekly for the first few months just to see how we were doing. In fact, I laugh about it now, but Craig will tell you that he was not interested in talking to Chris dur-ing this time, so he had Amy call many nights because he wasn't ready to talk to Chris. There was a ten-week period where Craig didn't talk to Chris. He needed some space to process all that had happened. The betrayal he felt as a leader and as the one who sought out Chris, brought him to Oklahoma, and bought into him as a pastor was overwhelming.

He wasn't perfect by any means, so he, too, needed to work through his pain and disappointment. However, despite all the feelings that were running rampant in his heart, he chose to bring restoration to our family regardless of how he felt. Knowing that Craig and Amy were fully supportive of our restoration process meant the world to Chris and me.

Craig and the church leadership were willing to walk us through this season, but they had stipulations that we had to follow. Chris answered to our church leadership for anything and everything. They told him the type of job he could get. And he listened. They came and took our family computer from our home for nearly two months. And Chris didn't argue. In fact, he willingly unplugged it and had it ready for them. He met with Jim as often as possible and heeded every word he said. He didn't make a decision without asking for advice. And the most powerful part of it all is that he walked through the doors of our church each and every Sunday morning. His head wasn't held too high, nor was he slouching over. He looked straight ahead, greeted those who hugged him and pressed on to become the best Christ follower, husband, and father he could. Few people do that when they've suffered a self-inflicted wound like his.

Many might think that such guidelines and rules would suffocate someone. Not in our case. We believe they were the very things that saved us. Craig and Amy's role was less invasive than Jim and Beth's, but their hearts were with us in prayer, and we knew it.

God's Favorite

The staff of LifeChurch.tv weren't the only ones to embrace Chris and me and pray us through the hard times. The campus we attended was a tremendous blessing as well. There was one person in particular whose belief in our restoration was nothing short of supernatural. It was as if she'd heard directly from God about us. In fact, I think she did.

It was April of 2002. I remember the day as if it were yesterday. Rita and I were sitting down to about as good a Tex-Mex lunch as you can find in Oklahoma. Even though things were on the mend between Chris and me, the pain was still fresh, and rarely a day went by when my cheeks weren't stained with tears. Some were sad tears. Some were happy tears. But they were tears nonetheless.

This precious friend had been in my life for less than a year. Truth be told, I can't explain why she and I bonded so very quickly—I'm young enough to be her daughter. But we connected right away, and I have such a deep love for this woman to this day.

As we were munching on some chips and salsa, she asked about my life. She probed into the deepest parts of my heart. She listened intently as if I were the most important person in the world to her. And during that lunch hour, I think I was. With each experience I shared, she shook her head in awe at how God had already worked miracles in my marriage. And when my eyes welled up with tears, so did hers.

As we were finishing our lunch together, I made every effort to put my feelings into words about what God was doing in my life. I finally said, "I feel like I'm God's favorite."

"You are. And I am too," she replied.

What?

In all my years of knowing Christ, it never dawned on me that I serve and love a God who can do anything and everything—including making each of His kids feel as if he or she is His personal favorite. His ability to go above and beyond our comprehension stuns me.

My time with Rita that day will forever stand out in my mind. Most onlookers would have just thought a couple of women were munching on some enchiladas and tacos. They would never have known that a young woman's heart was being molded by the Creator of the universe in an nondescript dining booth. And that He was using one of His children to do it.

I cannot remember a single finger pointed or eye rolled toward my husband and me. Just lots of smiles, "I'm prayin' for you," hugs, and "You're gonna make it" from individuals who truly believed they served a God who specializes in the impossible.

They were oh, so right.

Family Affair

When infidelity or unfaithfulness of any kind enters a relationship between a man and a woman, it doesn't take long before that wound extends to both sides of the family tree. It can become an intense, heated arena filled with opinions, advice, and more people to let down. Loyalties are torn and hearts are broken. But the alternative is to try living out your healing in secret. And that just doesn't work.

Probably the hardest moment for Chris, next to when he told me what happened, was the day he called his dad, Charles, to tell him the truth. Sons yearn for their dads' approval until the day they die. And Chris knew that what he had to share would deeply disappoint and sadden his dad. I sat there that evening and watched Chris admit his failure to the first man he ever loved. He wept like I'd never seen him weep before. But what made him cry even more was hearing the forgiving tone in his dad's voice. Charles was a true messenger of God's grace that night. And Chris needed that desperately.

Chris' five siblings were also very loving and gracious to Chris. They were heartbroken over what had happened and hoped that our family wouldn't dissolve because of his selfish actions. Chris' twin sister, Jenny, took it especially hard. She had a few words for him over the phone, but nothing that was ugly. Her disappointment was understandable because she and Chris had always been together. I almost wonder if she started carrying some of his pain for him during this time.

Telling my mother was something I was not looking forward to. I just knew she'd tell me to leave my marriage. Frankly, I wouldn't have blamed her. I might have given the same words to my child. But she didn't. In fact, even though she has given me plenty of advice, she refrained from doing so then.

I've always said that I would become a different person, almost a monster, if someone ever laid a hand on my sons and hurt them. I can't imagine the battle going on within her as she watched her baby girl's heart break into a million pieces. The problem was, I was 31 years old, and taking me to get a lollipop or candy bar at the store wasn't going to do the trick for this boo-boo.

My oldest brother, Mark, was very levelheaded about the situation. My dad was gone before I was married, so Chris asked Mark for my hand in marriage. Mark's reply was yes—with a strong admonition to take good care of me. I imagine Mark was angry that Chris did such a thing, but being an addict himself, Mark understands that addicts do things they never dreamed they'd ever do.

My biggest regret in our story is that I didn't immediately tell my brother David what happened. He was serving our country in Okinawa at the time, and our relationship just wasn't that strong. We didn't talk much because our lives were different, and we lived on two different continents. As you can imagine, when I finally told him more than a year later, he felt betrayed himself. He'd been in the military most of his adult life, and because of that, he was in many different places that took him far away from us. So my decision to withhold that information from him did nothing but intensify his feelings of being left out.

Hindsight is 20/20. If I knew then what I know now, I wouldn't have done that. I have learned that telling the truth is always the best policy, even if it makes someone uncomfortable or angry. At least that person will respect you for being forthcoming. Now, eight years later, my relationship with David is great. But I'm sorry I lost time with him.

Our families didn't have hands-on interaction with us during the first few fragile months, but they were behind us every step of the way. And today they know we are all part of a true miracle. They had every right to be angry at Chris. For them to tell me to walk away from my marriage would have been understandable. But they didn't. They prayed, loved, supported, encouraged, and modeled forgiveness better than any group of people I've ever seen.

The hardest part of going through something like this is telling someone. I believe that is why so many people feel alone in their pain. In their pride, anger, or embarrassment, they refuse to share their hurt with others. I understand this so well. Some of the hardest moments for me included pushing myself to do what every ounce of my flesh didn't want to do. I pushed through the pain, just praying that there was hope on the other side. I didn't go into a cave and hide myself from those who wanted to help me. I can't say I didn't think about it, but despite what everything inside me was crying out for, part of me—the part of me where the Holy Spirit lives—knew I had to submerge myself into hope. Hope given to me by the body of Christ.

I realize that the amount of support Chris and I received during this tumultuous situation is rare. Most people will say we are lucky to have this. Personally, we believe that God brought this support system to us to show us how it is supposed to be done. Our story was and is a very public one. We have a platform that allows us to demonstrate to other pastors and the entire body of Christ how to respond in the wake of such devastating news.

However, I believe that one of the reasons people don't have enough support when they are going through difficult times in their lives is that they don't open up their lives. I have spoken with many hurting people over the years, and when I ask if they have shared their story with someone or a small group of people, the answer is almost always no. Without opening up your heart to others, you will not heal. I'm utterly convinced of this. "Therefore confess your sins to each other and pray for each other so that you may be healed. The prayer of a righteous man is powerful and effective" (James 5:16).

You don't have to tell the whole world what has happened in your life the way Chris and I did. Some stories aren't going to be as public as ours. But if you are finding yourself in a heap of despair and don't see things getting any better, perhaps you haven't opened up your life to receive the kind of hope transplants that one can get through other like-minded believers.

Take a risk today. Share your heart.

And I believe, beyond a shadow of a doubt, that you will begin to experience true healing.

Your Healing Journey

1. When you are hurting, is your first response to share your pain with those you love or to push it away and ignore it?

2. Do you have a mentor in your life to whom you can go for godly counsel?

3. Why do some people have a difficult time reaching out for help?

4. Have you ever processed the deeper issues of life with others in a small group? If you've never had this experience, why haven't you?

5. If you are in pain right now and haven't shared it with someone close to you, will you take a step today and do it?

Whatever It Takes

I turned 40 years old in 2010.

Just seeing that fact in writing kind of makes my back hurt. However, to honor my life and this milestone, I set a goal to run my first 5K before I actually hit the big 4-0. I spent my school years running on the track team, but since then, I hadn't spent much time doing longer distances. I decided I wanted to add the 5K to my bucket list. So I did.

I awoke early the morning of the Oklahoma City Memorial Marathon in April 2010. It was a pleasant but chilly morning, and after I picked up my running partner, Amy, we were on our way downtown. We meandered our way through the streets to find thousands of other runners. Some were skilled marathoners who travel the country doing this for a living. Others, like me, were doing their very first race. It was crowded, people were pushing, and it was hard to find out where we were supposed to take off from. But it was certainly exhilarating. I could feel the adrenaline coursing through my veins. I had trained. I was ready.

Amy and I took off with all of the other runners and walkers. Most of the terrain was flat except for a couple of hills. We huffed and puffed up and down those hills, and before we knew it, the race was complete. I clocked my best time ever on those 3.1 miles, and we both felt like a million bucks. I was home by eight thirty that morning and definitely had a spring in my step the rest of the day. I actually ran a 5K without stopping at the age of 39.

Immediately my mind began to think about other races that maybe I could run. I could see myself doing a 10K. That would take more training, but I think I could handle it. What about a half-marathon? Could I really pull off 13.1 miles? I didn't even give a second thought to a marathon. I drive 26.2 miles, not run them. Running for five hours is not my idea of fun, even if it would get me a 26.2 sticker for the back of my car.

I learned something about myself after the race. Without a race in the future, I stopped running. I went a few weeks without running and realized that if I wanted to stay in shape, it might be good to set goals for myself. I honestly didn't want to though. I wanted to just sit on my porch, enjoy life, and not have to get up at the crack of dawn for boot camp or any other running activity. But my body won't stay fit and my heart won't stay healthy if I just sit. So I run.

To train for 5Ks and 10Ks, I get up early on Saturday mornings instead of sleeping in. I do toning and body sculpting on my own. I "carb up" on nights before the races. I hydrate before and after runs. I watch what I eat. I give my best effort to train for these events, but not because I want to accumulate dozens of stickers for my car or receive accolades from my friends. No, I do it because if I don't set some sort of goal in front of me, I probably won't run. And if I don't run, I'll sit. And if I sit, I won't be taking care of my body, which is the temple of the Holy Spirit. So I make the effort, work for something in the future (regardless of how uncomfortable it is), and expect to see amazing results.

Keeping a marriage healthy, even one that has not had a significant trauma, also requires training, maintenance, and goal setting. Doing what it takes when you actually feel like doing the opposite—*that* is what is required when you deeply care about something or someone.

Mending a Marriage

Some marriages won't survive infidelity. That's just reality.

They won't survive because wives and husbands don't want to endure the pain and discomfort that it takes to fix something that's broken. When your marriage is falling apart due to infidelity or any other betrayal, there will be nothing quick about the healing. It will take months and possibly years to reach an emotional, physical, spiritual, and mental place that feels anything close to normal.

Understandably, a person feels the pain of the initial betrayal so deeply that the idea of taking the difficult steps toward wholeness seems like signing on for more pain.

And that's not even the hard part.

The hard part is retraining your mind to do things differently this time around. Establishing new habits in your marriage as you relate to your spouse and others is an absolute must. Battling thoughts left and right as your spiritual enemy attempts to place obstacles in your way is par for the course. My friend Sarah says that we must divorce ourselves from our old marriages and start anew. She is so right.

Now, don't go thinking that I don't have faith. I've got faith. In fact, I've got plenty of it. And I'm totally convinced that God is able to do anything He desires. But He has given us humans a free will to make our own choices. And it's not altogether uncommon for us to royally mess things up, now is it?

Some people can't seem to forgive even though they've been forgiven of so much. Some people can't seem to walk in godly sorrow and do what it takes to win their spouse's trust back after betrayal. Some people can't admit they have a problem, and they want to ignore the pain and push it away. But of course, one day when they round the corner, it will still be there staring them smack-dab between the eyes. Some people just aren't willing to endure the pain and the effort to fix things. In my experience, this is just the way it is.

It Takes Two

Chris and I both feel very strongly that *restoring a marriage requires two people who are willing to do whatever it takes.* Whether infidelity or another betrayal has happened in marriage, only the "whatever it takes" mind-set and course of the heart will work. If only one person desires to see the relationship restored, the likelihood of that marriage surviving is slim. That's a hard pill to swallow, but from what I've seen in the other hurting marriages around me, it's true.

Take Steve, for example. He's a decent guy. He cares for his wife and children, but only to a certain extent. He hasn't said those words exactly, but his actions show nothing to the contrary. His issues run deep, and though he says he wants help and wants to be a better husband and father, he has proven otherwise. When issues arise that make his wife doubt, his defensive nature kicks in, and he wonders when she'll ever get over it. His marriage is being held together by a thread.

Then there is Kimberly. She got caught up in an inappropriate relationship that evolved into a full-blown affair. Instead of owning what she did and trying to make things right, she blamed her husband for all of it. If he had been more attentive to her, she wouldn't have looked elsewhere for the gratification she convinced herself she needed. Today, she and her husband are filing for divorce.

Neither of these situations exhibit the "whatever it takes" mentality that two partners must share in order to repair a damaged marriage. Throughout this book we've heard from several couples who did have and still do have this mind-set. Their marriages aren't perfect and never will be, but they are healthy and thriving, even after infidelity.

Sacrifices to Save the Marriage

When I tell people the things Chris and I have done over the years to make our marriage new, many are surprised. I rarely go out of town and leave Chris here by himself. Sometimes I do when he has the boys, but I don't spend a lot of time away from him. For me to leave him all alone for days on end could bring potential harm to him and to our marriage.

As I mentioned earlier, right after Chris' confession, we removed our computer so that the temptation and opportunity for him to visit pornographic websites would not be an obstacle to his healing in our home. A lot of people can't believe we did this because they can't imagine living without a computer. But Chris and I both understood that the computer wasn't merely a convenient tool for communication and research; it also provided direct access to pornography. When our minds shifted to this truth, there was no hesitation about what we had to do.

When we got the computer back, we put a password on it. Every time Chris wanted to get on the computer, I had to log him in.

We didn't have cable TV at the time, so that wasn't much of an issue for us. We did, however, enjoy renting movies. Do you know how hard it is to find a movie that doesn't have sexual content in it? So we typically watched cheesy movies or old movies, or we didn't watch anything at all.

It wasn't always convenient for me to do those things. At times I really wished things didn't have to be that way. But I made a commitment to my husband to do whatever it took to restore our marriage, and he made the same commitment to me. I chose to do things that were for him and for us and not just for me. These were sacrifices I willingly made for the healing of my marriage. I desperately desired to have a marriage that was better than ever. I was determined to do my part.

Some people have said that they don't think it's fair that I've had to do these things because of Chris' actions. Of course it's not fair! Life isn't fair. My pastor, Craig, says that sacrifice is giving up something you love for something you love more. So even though I enjoy doing things with my boys that might take us away from Chris, and even though I enjoy watching certain things on TV, those things don't mean nearly as much to me as my husband and my marriage.

Romans 5:8 says that "God demonstrates his own love for us in this: While we were still sinners, Christ died for us." I am happy that life isn't fair. I'm happy that I don't get what I deserve. I'm happy for the mercy and grace bestowed upon me by my heavenly Father.

Feeding Your Spirit

In Romans 7, Paul describes our struggle with making good choices. He says in verse 15, "I do not understand what I do. For what I want to do I do not do, but what I hate I do. And if I do what I do not want to do, I agree that the law is good."

Isn't that just the way it is?

I know you've been there. I can't imagine any honest people saying they've truly been able to make good choices and deny their flesh every moment of every day. We mustn't fool ourselves: The flesh is strong. And that's exactly what Paul is talking about. If we just needed to make and keep a decision, we could probably do it. We humans have enough willpower (most of the time) to do something we feel strongly about. But then the flesh comes in and says, "Oh, you can have that piece of chocolate cake today. One piece won't hurt." Those who struggle with food issues know that one piece turns into more. So what do we do with this? As Christ followers, how do we overcome our flesh when every part of it is screaming at us to keep doing what feels so good but is so wrong?

We feed our spirits.

When we nurture our souls with the truth of God, we are built up. We want to follow Him. We want to serve Him. I have found this to be so true in my own life. When I am spending time in God's Word, meditating on His truth, praying for those closest to me and others I don't know, and worshipping God by singing or playing the piano, I am feeding my spirit. The more I focus on the Spirit, the more my flesh calms down.

The contrary is true as well. The more I try to deny my flesh and ignore my desires, the more I focus on denying my flesh and missing the things I think I need. Then I usually succumb to my fleshly desires and cave headfirst into whatever it is that I am trying to steer clear of.

The Bible says in Luke 9:23, "Then [Jesus] said to them all: 'If anyone would come after me, he must deny himself and take up his cross daily and follow me.'" Denying ourselves, our flesh, is absolutely biblical, and it's what we are called to do if we are truly following Christ. But I am suggesting that you and I stop focusing on denying the flesh and focus instead on feeding our spirits. In turn, I believe, we will indeed deny the flesh. It's all about our focus.

Denying ourselves and doing what we are called to do is often extremely hard, especially when we are repairing our marriages. Sometimes the pain is so awful and the wound is so deep that we can't even imagine getting to the other side of it, let alone actually having a great life afterward. But it is possible.

When a Spouse Stands Alone

I have many friends who have walked the road that Chris and I have. In some cases, both spouses were willing to lay down their lives and work hard to resuscitate the marriage. Some were not. God is amazing at restoration, and He is also quite brilliant with new beginnings.

My good friend Kaci went through a tumultuous ordeal in her marriage many years back. She learned that her husband had adulterous affairs that pretty much lasted their entire marriage. You can try to imagine what she felt like, but you probably won't succeed (unless you've been there). That kind of devastation is hard to take in. The lost years, the wasted moments, and the stolen dreams were all she could think about. And her children.

They tried to make it work for a little while. But her husband didn't fight the fight for very long and eventually fell into a full-blown adulterous lifestyle that left his family spinning. All Kaci ever wanted was to serve God with her husband and love their children. That's not too much to ask, is it?

Kaci's husband had already walked away from the marriage, so one might think that once Kaci made the decision to end the marriage, she would have peace and hope. That was definitely not the case. In fact, watching her walk through it was heart wrenching because I knew what it was doing to her and to her children. The aftermath of her husband's choices was downright ugly.

But eventually they got divorced and had to figure out the schedules for their children. Kaci went on to do her best as a newly divorced mom, juggling many responsibilities. Meanwhile, her ex-husband continued in his way of life, not seeming to have a care for anyone but himself. The gratification of his flesh was his sole focus. I haven't seen an uglier story.

But then God did His thing.

After some time and a lot of soul-searching and praying, Kaci and her children bounced back. They weren't pain free by any means, but they'd chosen to keep their eyes fixed on their Savior and to allow Him to bring healing to their wounded hearts. And He did.

He also brought someone else to them. A new husband and dad. The children still spent time with their father, but they didn't seem to be a priority in his life. So having a man who was vested in their days and futures turned out to be a big blessing. Kaci never could have imagined this happening in the throes of her pain and devastation.

I keep up with Kaci on a regular basis. Our hearts will always be knit together because we saw each other at our worst moments. She saw what Chris and I went through, and I saw what she endured. Two similar stories with two very different endings. The effects of Kaci's ex-husband's choices still linger, but there are so many good things happening. I asked Kaci to share from her heart about where she is now, and here is what she said.

> We have been blessed by God, but that has not meant "smooth" anything. Life has been full of difficult challenges, and my ex continually places the children in harmful situations. Thankfully, God has seen me through so many tough and agonizing places that I can trust Him with my children. The firm truth I walk in daily is that if something tragic happens to the kids, God will see us through even that. I used to pray that God would keep those bad things from happening, but now I know deep in my heart that no matter what, God will be present with them and me, and we will walk through each experience with Him.
>
> I guess that is my story. So often we Christians want everything tied up with a pretty bow, but life is just too messy. I do love my life and my new husband. I am blessed and treated like a princess, so I'm experiencing what my

heart had always longed for in a relationship. I am able to model struggle, challenges, and restoration. My kids have open communication with me, and we walk along our journey together. They have so much compassion and empathy for others that there are times I thank God for all the tragedy we have suffered. But they also struggle with my husband's "amazingness" because it is a constant and painful reminder of how far off their dad is. Overall, we have constant challenges that when examined closely would break my heart. So I choose the "big picture" approach and trust God with the details!

Kaci's ex-husband wasn't willing to do whatever it takes. He said the words at first and even made a few grand strides, but in the end, he chose to please himself. He chose to walk away from his family and dive into his new lifestyle, and the ripple effect has continued for years. But just because that happened doesn't mean God wasn't there. You read what Kaci wrote. God was and is there with them, and He has changed her heart and the hearts of her children.

Advice from the Heart

No matter where you are in life, God will meet you there. I'd love to be able to tell you that He will keep all harm from coming across your path. He certainly is capable of doing so, but if you've been through any pain in your life, you know He doesn't always do that. Rarely do awful circumstances gracefully adorn our paths. No, they come whirling, twirling, and rampaging onto our horizons like a tornado.

But please don't underestimate the power of our God as His Spirit works through willing individuals to resuscitate even the worst of circumstances. He is fully able and willing. Fully. The million-dollar question is, are you?

I give a lot of advice and counsel to people, mainly because they ask. This is funny to me because I don't have any areas of expertise attached to my name. You won't see Cindy Beall, PhD; Cindy Beall,

CEO; or Cindy Beall, EdD. The only initials I have next to my name are MRS. And I guess that's fitting because it's my marriage story that has prompted people to ask me so many questions.

So take this piece of advice with a grain of salt: Be willing to do whatever it takes to make the marriage work, or let each other go.

Your Healing Journey

1. Have you ever trained to accomplish a goal? Share or write down your experiences and how the discipline of training made you feel.

2. Even if you aren't the betrayer in the marriage, do you believe you have to make sacrifices to mend your situation? What is required of each spouse?

3. Cindy mentions feeding your spirit. What are some ways you can feed your spirit and, as a result, see your flesh starve?

4. If you've have marriage struggles, are you willing to do whatever it takes to mend your marriage? Why or why not?

~~~~~~~~~~~~~~~~~~~~~~~~~~~~~

A Story of Healing in Their Own Words

~~~~~~~~~~~~~~~~~~~~~~~~~~~~~

JIM AND BETH

THE FIRST TIME I MET BETH, I INSULTED HER. And Beth, in her true "Beth" fashion, just laughed and laughed as I continued to make a very good fool of myself. I clearly didn't realize at the time that I was saying something derogatory about her church background, but I was. Little did I know that several months later, I'd need her more than ever because this Jim and Beth is *our* Jim and Beth—the couple who traveled with us along our very disturbing road of infidelity.

They had their own road of infidelity to walk down and eventually push through when Chris and I were just children. Jim and Beth will tell you that it took major effort to be where they are today, but they are so thankful that they endured the pain to have what they have now. And that was nearly 30 years ago.

Here is a great opportunity for you to hear from their hearts about all they went through.

⸰

CINDY: Beth, what was your initial response when you found out about Jim's infidelity?

BETH: I was nine months pregnant with our daughter. He confessed to me over the phone, and he let me know that I was free to get a divorce if that was what I wanted. I went through the whole range of emotions more often than I would have ever dreamed.

CINDY: Jim, did you ever think you'd "do such a thing" as commit adultery?

JIM: Growing up I was taught that if a person committed adultery, he could never marry another person or he would lose his salvation. That was a motivator for me not to consider ever crossing that line. I never even seriously considered it until a few hours before I actually did commit adultery. I began to rationalize my situation and decided to take my chances with my eternal destination.

CINDY: Beth, what happened that made you decide to stay?

BETH: I called Jim when our daughter, Emily, was ten days old, and I asked him to come get me and bring me home. And he did! Almost immediately after Jim's phone confession, I began to ask God to show me if I had a part in all of this. In and out of the pain and challenges of the circumstances, I began to see that I had shortcomings myself and that I needed to focus on my own issues, not on Jim's. It was a humbling time, and I surrendered to whatever God would do in the marriage.

CINDY: Jim, how have you dealt with the pain you've seen in Beth's eyes over the years?

JIM: This will sound unbelievable to most, but I don't remember seeing pain in her eyes beyond the first year after I was unfaithful. That has been almost 30 years ago. She has never brought up my unfaithfulness in any conversation or conflict. Never. Now we openly share our experience with others and talk about my actions, but she has never used my adultery as leverage in an argument or an opportunity to bring shame.

CINDY: Beth, how have you been able to forgive Jim?

BETH: Forgiving was a process for me. But I just had to forgive myself and him and trust God to do the rest. That's hard when you are someone who likes to be in control.

CINDY: Jim, do you ever find yourself walking in shame because of what you did? What does living in brokenness mean for you?

JIM: I am very sad for what I did. However, I turned my sadness for my actions into resolve to be the servant-leader my wife deserved. Her example of forgiveness was a real-life reminder of the grace of God and His forgiveness. I embrace the story of the life of David and see that his sin of adultery did not separate him from a loving God—he is even called a man after God's own heart! The forgiveness that God extended David and the forgiveness that my wife extended me have made it possible for me to live without shame and to live with incredible thankfulness for the grace given to me.

I don't deserve the grace and forgiveness I received. I know I'm still capable of the sin of adultery. I embrace my brokenness and strive to live with humility and a willingness to serve and forgive others.

CINDY: What about trust?

BETH: I decided to trust God first and release Jim to God. I still do that today.

JIM: I try to do all I can to let her know that she has complete access to every part of my life. My cell phone, laptop, wallet, mail, plans for the day, relationships at work, and anything that I would consider personal is available to her to ask questions about or ask to see. I knew that I would need to go above and beyond what would seem reasonable to rebuild trust. All the things I originally put in place to assure her that I was trustworthy are still in place today, 30 years later.

CINDY: How is your marriage today?

BETH: Our marriage today is good—better than ever. Every day is a new day with the realization that I have such a special gift in a man who has incredible wisdom and a godly character. We just celebrated our thirty-eighth wedding anniversary, and I'm grateful for the challenges we have experienced along the way because they helped shape us and break us of ourselves so we could help others. God has redeemed us, restored us, and empowered us to provide the generations that follow with an example of surrendered commitment.

JIM: We are in our fifties, and my heart still jumps a little when I see her. I believe we are experiencing what the Bible calls being one. The oneness we have is difficult to describe in words, as is our oneness with Christ. But we have it, and it is incredible. It was not without trials and challenges and pain and tears and breaking and shaping, but it is worth it all. We are *one*. Beth is my best friend, and it seems to get better every day.

Now do you see why God handpicked Jim and Beth to walk us through the darkest time in our lives? They are absolutely incredible and the real deal. I cannot even find the words to express my gratitude for their input, advice, counsel, wisdom, love, support, and generosity all these years. Even today, their influence in our life is present. In fact, I've probably thanked them a few dozen times over the years, and I still don't think it's enough. So Jim and Beth, thank you. From the bottom of my heart, thank you.

11

Should I Stay, or Should I Go?

I WOULD LOVE TO BE ABLE TO GIVE an absolute answer when people ask me if they should stay in their broken marriages. A simple yes or no would make your decision so much easier, but it just doesn't work that way. You are the one who has to live with your choice. And at the end of the day, I will probably sleep soundly on my memory-foam pillow and not give too much thought to your decision because the decision is between you and God.

I remember this season in my life. This question began to plague me almost immediately after Chris' confession. Within a very short time, I pictured myself as a single mom who would be headed back to work while trying to figure out how to share the parenting with my unfaithful husband. Not only that, but I figured I would need financial help from my family to do it, which would be more humiliating than I thought I could handle.

I don't know why I felt I had to decide the future of my marriage within hours of the startling revelation that it was dead. Maybe I didn't want to waste any more time than I already had. Maybe I didn't want to be fooled one more day. Maybe I wanted to have some sense of control of the journey ahead. In my mind, our nine years of marriage was just a sham. A smokescreen. Nothing real. Nothing meaningful. Did I really want to stay with someone who clearly didn't cherish me? Didn't I deserve someone who actually would?

A few days after Chris' confession, two of our pastors, Jerry and Kevin, came over to talk with us. I remember vaguely talking about what happened and the future and how I felt and what I was going to do. They both listened, and I'm certain they could hear the panic in my voice. I remember telling them that I wasn't sure what I should do. Very gently Kevin replied, "You don't have to make that decision today."

And he was absolutely right.

In fact, his simple eight-word sentence was the best piece of advice I received during that time. It instantly brought me peace and comfort. In order to hear from God about my future, I needed to be free from the thoughts that were beginning to overwhelm me. The burden of my future had been lifted off my back. The truth was, I didn't have to know that day or the next week or even the next month. There was no wisdom in deciding the rest of my life within days of the biggest, most devastating piece of news I've ever received. It just wasn't smart. So I waited.

Thanks, Kevin.

How Wisdom Can Be Yours

I was an average student in all of my classes—except for Spanish. I did well, and secretly I felt pretty smart about taking Spanish. After all, we lived in central Texas, and our southern neighbor was Mexico. So while others chose German or French or even Latin (Latin? Really?), I realized that I showed some inkling of intelligence by my choice of a foreign language. But those moments of confidence in my choices and abilities were rare.

When I ventured off to college at Texas State University in San Marcos (formerly Southwest Texas State University), I followed in the footsteps of my parents. I received my bachelor's degree in elementary education one December afternoon in 1993. It was one of the best days of my life.

But despite that accomplishment, I always felt as if everyone in my family was smarter than me. My brothers are both incredibly smart, and I wondered why academics came so naturally for them but not for me.

Then there is my husband. The man is so smart it makes your head spin. And not just in the book sense, but in the "I may not know the answer right this minute, but give me a few hours to research the question and I'll come up with a stellar response" kind of way. To make matters worse, when he learns something, he actually retains it. Why, Lord? The man I married is practically a genius.

Knowing that, you can understand my feelings of insecurity at the beginning of our marriage. The only thing I had on him was that I could recall my Spanish lessons and say rude or condescending things to him when I was frustrated, and he wouldn't know it as long as I had a smile on my face. (What? You wouldn't do that?)

Then one day, I stumbled upon a verse in the book of James that hit me like a ton of textbooks. I'd read through James many times, but on this day, I barely got into the first chapter before the fifth verse leapt off the page at me: "If any of you lacks wisdom, he should ask God, who gives generously to all without finding fault, and it will be given to him."

That was it! My ticket to intelligence would come through my heavenly Father and His Word. I no longer had to worry about my ability (or lack thereof) to know something. It's as if the lightbulb came on in that instant and illuminated my dimly lit mind. Almost instantly I began uttering a simple prayer that I still pray to this day: "God, please give me wisdom beyond my years."

Knowledge and intelligence are often applauded in our world. Scholarships and awards go to the brightest, most intelligent minds. And that's not a bad thing by any means, but those who struggle with understanding algebraic formulas will never have such a trophy to adorn their living room shelves.

But with God, the ability to gain insight and understanding is at your fingertips. Actually, it's more like on the tip of your tongue. A simple prayer can open up a world of opportunity. I know this well.

Am I a Bible scholar? Clearly I am not. I haven't received any seminary training. The only thing remotely close to that is spending time with amazing Bible teachers like Kay Arthur and Beth Moore over the years as they've taught the Word of God to me. (Well, it wasn't like we were discussing it over coffee or anything. But maybe someday…)

Covenant 101

Before I give you my personal opinion based on the Word of God, let's establish some common ground. Whether someone is leaning toward staying or going, those of us who find ourselves dealing with infidelity must realize that the covenant of our marriage vows has been broken. For whatever reason, God in His sovereignty said that the act of infidelity would break that covenant.

> It has been said, "Anyone who divorces his wife must give her a certificate of divorce." But I tell you that anyone who divorces his wife, except for marital unfaithfulness, causes her to become an adulteress, and anyone who marries the divorced woman commits adultery (Matthew 5:31-32).

People are as different as night and day. We have different dreams, ideas, thoughts, beliefs, morals…you name it. But those of us who call ourselves Christ followers ought to have the same standard: the Bible. God's inspired Word.

Call me simple or elementary, but when I read these two verses in Matthew, I read that God does permit divorce when there is marital unfaithfulness. Over the years, I've heard many well-meaning people who have absolutely no idea what it's like to endure infidelity say that God still hates divorce and doesn't permit it—ever.

'Scuse me? Really?

Then why on earth is the exception for adultery mentioned in Matthew 5? Did the Creator of the universe make a mistake? Did Matthew hear God incorrectly? No. God didn't make an error, and Matthew's hearing was just fine. I believe wholeheartedly that God knows the seriousness of unfaithfulness in the marriage relationship. He tells us to save ourselves for our spouses and not to give in to sexual immorality.

By no means am I suggesting that people should just throw in the towel when their spouse has been unfaithful to them. That's clearly not my story. I'm all about fighting to save your marriage when the fight is in *both* of you. It's hard to restore a marriage on a good day when both are willing to fight. It's nearly dreadful if only one person is committed. Or so I've seen.

Having shared that verse, I should provide some commentary to put behind those words. Here is some information I found in my *NIV Life Application Bible.*

> Jesus said that divorce is not permissible except for unfaithfulness. This does not mean that divorce should automatically occur when a spouse commits adultery. The word translated "unfaithfulness" implies a sexually immoral lifestyle, not a confessed and repented act of adultery. Those who discover that their partner has been unfaithful should first make every effort to forgive, reconcile, and restore their relationship. We are always to look for reasons to restore the marriage relationship rather than for excuses to leave it.[4]

Did you see that part? Unfaithfulness doesn't mean an act of adultery followed by repentance. Clearly this is someone's opinion, but I think there is something to be said for it.

I've known many couples who have had to walk this road. Some of their marriages ended. Some have been restored and are now thriving. Others are just stagnant and not making any progress.

Take my friend Erin for example. Her husband, Andy, began an unhealthy relationship with a coworker years ago. Erin found out and was just crushed. Andy responded by making a 180-degree turnaround.

He left his job and began to make changes immediately. He owned his sin and didn't make excuses for what he'd done. After a lot of tears and questions and also some counseling, they are now stronger than ever. Andy truly repented. Erin truly forgave.

Not all situations turn out so well. My friend Susan endured the same thing with her husband, Kevin. They were serving the Lord together and were blessed with terrific children. One day Kevin came clean about his sin and unloaded all of it on Susan. Devastation set in for her immediately. At first he appeared to be repentant and willing to make their marriage work. But over the course of many months, the truth became known—he did not want to leave his second life behind. Kevin was not repentant and continued in his sin. Susan filed for divorce.

I've heard people say that they are afraid they will be punished for the rest of their lives if they get a divorce. Wow, really? That's not the God I love and know. The God I adore and have pledged to serve as long as there is breath in my lungs is a forgiving and loving God who wants the very best for His children. He forgives all sin. He loves all people. He even forgives divorce. He even loves the divorcee. Even when the divorce shouldn't have happened.

Are there difficulties that will occur due to divorce? Yes. We call those *consequences*. And they come with every sin we commit. But make no mistake about it: God is bigger than any sin and any consequences and can bring blessing out of even the most dreadful circumstances. It's what He does. It's who He is.

Both Erin and Susan are living wonderfully blessed lives today. Erin stayed with her husband, and now their marriage is thriving. Better than ever. Susan chose to walk away (after giving it all she could, mind you), and years later is now married to a man who truly cherishes her and her children. Erin and Susan are still dealing with consequences of their husbands' sins in different ways. That's just the way sin is. But both are walking in the blessing of trusting God with their lives.

We so easily discard things in our world, including marriages. Many don't truly take the wedding vows seriously. The moment any terrible situation arises in our relationship with our spouse, we are tempted to take off. Jump ship. Call it quits. Not everyone, but there are plenty who do.

I believe in doing everything we possibly can to restore a broken or dead marriage. Many will say that is an impossible feat. And for some situations, it just might be.

When I share what has happened in my marriage, almost always the response is, "I don't know if I could forgive something like that." That's understandable. It is awful. There is the daunting task of forgiveness looking you square in the eyes. Not to mention the tremendous ongoing mental effort you have to exert to get through the pain of images that bombard your ever-lovin' mind. I know. Oh, I know.

Now, correct me if I'm wrong, but the last time I checked, our God is bigger than any other force that might seek to contaminate our minds. Let's not forget who we say we serve. "With man this is impossible, but with God all things are possible" (Matthew 19:26).

What I Do Know

From the beginning of Chris' and my story, we have shouted from the rooftops, "It takes two people to be willing to do whatever it takes to make a marriage work." And nine years later, we are still standing on that soapbox.

If you ever find yourself in shoes that are either pointed for the door to walk away or pointed toward your spouse to stay, pray for God to tell you what to do. He will. I don't know what the answer will be, but I do know that God does. Get counsel from godly people in your life, pray, and know that ultimately you have to live with the decision you make.

I also know that my God is absolutely the Creator of the universe. He is infinitely wiser and more loving than we could ever dream. His power reaches into the galaxies, the stars are His handiwork, and the earth is His footstool. Nothing is too difficult for Him.

But He is also a gentleman. He doesn't force us to follow Him or love Him. And there will be some men and women who choose to live in a place of hard-heartedness. Many of you have experienced this firsthand, and because of that, your marriage ended. But you're still blessed, aren't you? Because that's the way God rolls.

Your Healing Journey

1. Based on Matthew 5:31-32, do you believe divorce is ever permitted? Why or why not?

2. Why are many people so quick to jump to divorce as an option for a troubled marriage?

3. If you are making a choice, how are you going about gathering wisdom and help to prepare for the decision?

4. How does looking at the importance of covenant shape the way you look at marriage? At God? At your own relationship with Christ?

5. You will hear many opinions from many people, but you have to rely on God and your heart—as does your spouse. How are you really feeling? How are you feeling led? These might be in conflict, so pay attention to God's leading.

12

Guarding Your Heart, Guarding Your Marriage

I GREW UP THE DAUGHTER OF two schoolteachers, which basically translates that I didn't come from money. When my mother and I shopped for clothes, we typically headed straight to the clearance racks to find the bargains. There was no full-price purchasing going on in the Moehring family. That's for certain.

Almost all of our family vacations consisted of going camping. Most of my vacation memories have a camper and a lake involved. (If you go camping in Texas in the summer, there must be a lake.) At the age of 11, I finally got my wobbly, scrawny legs to hold me up on water skis.

Water skiing became a favorite activity for my brothers and me. During the summers, my brothers slept in late unless we were going skiing. There is nothing quite as satisfying for a water skier as cutting across on a lake that is smooth as glass. The cool, crisp mornings provided that opportunity for us.

One doesn't ski for hours on end. Being up on your skis for three or four minutes can zap your energy. If you've done any water skiing yourself, you know how exhausting it is. So after we all had a round of skiing, we'd throw our life jackets on, float in the middle of the lake, and get rested before another trip around the lake.

An unexpected thing happened one day during that time of relaxation. After several minutes of floating, we looked around and realized we were no longer in the middle of the lake. None of us had been aware of what was happening. We didn't feel it. Yet we discovered that because our boat wasn't anchored, we gradually drifted.

Foundations that Hold Strong

In order for us to remain stable and strong and to avoid drifting in our spiritual lives, we have to anchor ourselves to something that won't change. We must be unmovable when the winds of change and compromise come. (And trust me, they will come.) To change our analogy from water to land, we need a firm foundation. My heart's desire is to stand on what I know is truth when all things around me are vying for my attention and devotion. I've learned in my 40 years of life that my foundation won't be strong unless I'm spending ample time in Bible study, prayer, and worship.

Daily routines such as Bible study, journaling, and prayer have become increasingly difficult over the years for me. While writing this book, I am working part-time as a bookkeeper, managing my home, and being a wife to my pastor husband and a mom to my very busy boys. Because of that, I don't get a lot of time to just sit and submerge my mind in God's Word the way I could when my life was simpler. So I must make an effort to spend a little time here and there. I've become a thief lately by stealing moments away from my hectic lifestyle in order to strengthen my foundation. I try to memorize a Scripture that applies to where I am in my life journey. I play music that keeps my focus on Christ.

I also try to limit how much of the world is coming into my mind. I make every attempt to ignore the latest rumors of Brad and Angelina while I'm waiting in line at the grocery store. You may think that trivial, but I beg to differ. If Satan gets an inch, he'll try to take a mile. We must be on our guard against forces that would weaken our foundation. I pray up and gear up for war. Not a physical war, but a war in the mind.

> Finally, be strong in the Lord and in his mighty power. Put on the full armor of God so that you can take your stand against the devil's schemes. For our struggle is not against flesh and blood, but against the rulers, against the authorities, against the powers of this dark world and against the spiritual forces of evil in the heavenly realms. Therefore put on the full armor of God, so that when the day of evil comes, you may be able to stand your ground, and after you have done everything, to stand. Stand firm then, with the belt of truth buckled around your waist, with the breastplate of righteousness in place, and with your feet fitted with the readiness that comes from the gospel of peace. In addition to all this, take up the shield of faith, with which you can extinguish all the flaming arrows of the evil one. Take the helmet of salvation and the sword of the Spirit, which is the word of God. And pray in the Spirit on all occasions with all kinds of prayers and requests (Ephesians 6:10-18).

I imagine Paul wrote this letter to the church at Ephesus because they were being caught off guard. Chances are that the Ephesians were just like you and me, going about their way when all of a sudden they were slammed with a circumstance that threw them off kilter. That sort of thing happens to us all. I think we can all say, "Yep, been there, done that, got the T-shirt."

Awareness of Weaknesses

Most of the time, our challenges come at us gradually. It's seduction at its finest, really. I've never had a man walk up to me and ask me to go to a hotel with him to engage in sexual activity. If that were to ever happen, I would probably laugh and say, "Nice try, Satan" and walk away. It wouldn't have interested me in the slightest. That's not my gig. I suppose there are encounters that might happen that way, but I've learned that the tactics of our spiritual enemy are far more subtle than that.

When Chris and I were at a previous church, there was a man who gave compliments to me almost every time he saw me. He would tell me how nice I sang or how pretty I was or that I was a wonderful person. At the time this was happening, the distance between Chris and me was broadening by the minute. I didn't know what was happening in his life. All I knew is that the Grand Canyon was forming between us. My need for Chris' admiration, love, support, and devotion was at an all-time high. He was not fulfilling those needs, so I allowed this man to do so with his kind words.

Nothing ever happened. There were never any phone calls, e-mails, or other secret communications between him and me. It was just when I saw him at church events. I'm ashamed to admit that I looked forward to seeing him. I made sure I was wearing something cute or that my hair was adorned a certain way. I was starving for attention from my husband, and when he didn't provide it, I willingly received it from this man. Thankfully, this man never made any suggestions to me about a physical encounter. (If that's not an example of "There, but for the grace of God, go I," I don't know what is.)

Peter gives us an eye-opening description of what Satan does on a daily basis. He's out there. He's just waiting to find someone who is not paying close attention. When he sees an opening, he strikes: "Be self-controlled and alert. Your enemy the devil prowls around like a roaring lion looking for someone to devour" (1 Peter 5:8).

Satan would have loved nothing more than for me to give in to those compliments from the man who was not my husband. In fact, the more I think about it, the more I realize that I could have easily gone down that path had I not realized what was happening. But I did pay attention. I knew that although my husband was physically present in my life, he was emotionally absent for a long period of time. Many would say that it's understandable that I would have found a counterfeit source to meet my needs. But that's not the standard I hold myself to. I firmly believe that even when others sin against us, we don't have license to sin back. When we get revenge or try to play a part in others "getting what they deserve," we are sinning against God and breaking His heart first and foremost.

During this time I told my trusted friend Ana-María what was happening. She was concerned for my marriage and me and was faithful to join forces and pray. She also held me accountable. That was key. She challenged me to honor the covenant I made and encouraged me with the truth of God's Word. Eventually, I began to fill my mind with things of God and allowed God to become the husband I needed emotionally.

I couldn't avoid the man altogether, but I managed to have very few contacts with him. When we did see each other and he said something nice, I literally began to feel sick. The compliments became unattractive to me, and I no longer desired hearing them, nor did I make an effort to see him. What's interesting is that this man wasn't drop-dead gorgeous or anything like that. I wasn't even really attracted to him. But I was attracted to what he was saying to me.

It was extremely hard work to fight that battle. To pay such close attention to the spiritual attack that was all around me sometimes took every bit of my energy. Sometimes I just wanted to sit down and do nothing. But I had to take the high road because even in the midst of it all, I realized what was at stake. So I made the choice to feed my spirit, which in turn caused my flesh to starve.

Only when you are aware of your weaknesses, your longings, and your unmet needs can you strive for healthy healing answers like God's leading, connections with your spouse, and accountability with friends. By feeding your spirit and knowing yourself, you can overcome the temptations that can and will come your way.

Take time to examine your heart. It's amazing—we long to have our significant other know us intimately and truly, and yet many of us have not done the work to uncover our true selves and needs. No wonder we blame the other person when something does go wrong. But in the end, it isn't a whole, abundant life. Get to know yourself—you just might discover many other exciting wonders and dreams in that heart of yours.

Just Having Fun or Playing with Fire?

My husband and I had a single friend with whom we were really close years ago. He wasn't just Chris' friend; he really was my friend too. We met him together. Eventually, he began to come see us quite often—like every other weekend. We truly enjoyed his company, and he became like family to us. He was like a brother to Chris and to me.

Our friend was a night owl, and at the time, so was I. Chris often went to bed early, and this friend and I would stay up at night just talking. We talked mostly about Jesus and ministry and his future wife. There was no flirting or anything inappropriate going on. At the time, I didn't give it a second thought. But now? Now I realize how foolish it was and how easily we could have gotten involved because we were "sharing our hearts." What an idiot I was.

You may be doing that exact thing right now. In fact, a woman once commented on my blog that she and her husband share a best friend. The friend is a guy, and they both do things with him. She went on to say that nothing would ever happen and that her husband trusts her completely.

"Danger, Will Robinson!"

Really? When you are married, spending one-on-one time with someone of the opposite sex or someone of the same sex who might find you attractive is *never* a good idea. No, it's not. It can be easy to rationalize, to temper concern with logical reasons, and to wave common sense away with "Nothing would ever happen." But as we've seen in each personal story, most people who have affairs never planned to. Creating this "rule" isn't about rules. It's about protecting your heart and your marriage with the same love and care with which you tend to anything that matters to you—and with wisdom and every precaution available to you.

I want you to know why I am so passionate about this. As I look back at my life, I realize that I was one slippery step away from falling into a full-fledged affair on more than one occasion.

Protect What You Love

If you are a parent, you know that the love you feel for your children is indescribable. It's a love you've never experienced. This love can cause more pain in your heart and more joy than you could imagine—within moments of each other. It's powerful and oftentimes all-consuming.

I'm 100 percent certain that I would do anything to protect my sons. If any force ever attempted to bring harm to their lives, I would step in. I would literally lay down my life for theirs. Does that mean I'm suicidal? No, it means I care, and if circumstances called for me to make the ultimate sacrifice, I would.

I can also tell you that if someone was threatening my boys' lives in any way, I'd take that person out. Does that mean I'm a murderer? No, it just means that I will protect my boys. I am not likely to ever need to use deadly force, but the capability is very much there, depending on the happenings in my life.

We must be on our guard and realize that given the right conditions in life, we are capable of just about anything—for good or for evil. Our circumstances can heavily influence our actions. In addition, we have a very real enemy. Whether you choose to admit that or not is up to you.

Regardless of your opinion on spiritual warfare, the Bible is clear: Satan's mission statement is to steal from you, kill you, and destroy you. He will seek to accomplish this by any means necessary. He is not on your side, though he will try to convince you he is. His gentle whispers to your mind are laced with deceit. They may sound attractive. They may even sound as if he is trying to make your life better. Trust me, he's not.

Why Guidelines Matter

When Chris and I realized how much our external circumstances can influence our choices, thoughts, and ongoing behaviors, we did what many other couples we know have done—we set up guidelines in our marriage. These guidelines protect our marriages and our integrity as individuals and as God's children.

For example, we make sure we aren't alone with individuals of the opposite sex. This issue is hard to deal with in certain circles. If you mention that you have this guideline when people stop by to visit, they might get defensive, as if you are accusing them of having impure motives, of being the "affair type." People might automatically think, "So you think I want to start an affair with you right now?"

Good grief.

No. That's not the way it works. People cross the line gradually, and I want to make sure I don't put myself in situations where something like this might happen in the future. My heart is for Mr. Chris Beall, and I want to make sure I save it for him and him alone. No other man needs even a piece of it.

I correspond with men by e-mail on a regular basis. And when I do, I make sure to write only what I would be comfortable with my husband reading. In fact, quite often I will mention my husband in the e-mail and might even end it with something like "Chris and I appreciate you," or "Chris and I will pray for you." These are subtle reminders that we are a united couple.

I also give my husband full access to my e-mail and social media accounts. Recently I briefly corresponded with an old boyfriend from high school. He sent a short message to me on Facebook, and I responded to him. I felt the need to do so because the message from him was an apology, and I wanted him to know that I had no hard feelings over the past. He proceeded to tell me about a bad situation with one of his children, and I assured him that I would pray for his son. I showed the entire communication to my husband and made sure to write only what I felt comfortable showing my husband. Since that time, there has been no more correspondence.

It's not that we shouldn't or won't ever communicate with someone of the opposite sex; it's that we need to be wise when we do so.

Be On Your Game

I love college football, especially when the Texas Longhorns are playing. (Hook 'em.) Born and raised in Texas and growing up just north of Austin, I love the color burnt orange. And if you know anything about college football rivalries, you will understand when I tell you that I live in hostile territory between August and December each year.

I live in Oklahoma. You know, where the wind comes sweeping down the plain? And the home of the Sooners is just 45 minutes south of my home. A large amount of smack talk can be heard in this area during the football season. People do their best to get a rise out of us, but Chris and I endure it and believe we are stronger for it. (Blessed are those who are persecuted for righteousness.) Ahem.

But I rarely smack talk, even when my boys are ranked in the top five or when they are undefeated. Why? Because anything is possible in college football. Over the years, we've endured some of the biggest upsets that have ever occurred.

Anything is possible in the ultimate game of life as well, and the stakes are much higher. So never say never, and prepare your heart and build up the right muscles in preparation for the possible challenges that could come your way.

I'm as loyal as the day is long. Sometimes to a fault. But you and I must choose to be on guard for the upsets and the unexpected.

‹œ›x‹œ›x‹œ›x‹œ›x‹œ›x‹œ›x‹œ›x‹œ›x‹œ›x‹œ››

A Story of Healing in Their Own Words

‹œ›x‹œ›x‹œ›x‹œ›x‹œ›x‹œ›x‹œ›x‹œ›x‹œ›x‹œ››

CHAD AND SARAH

SARAH IS ONE OF MY FAVORITE WRITERS. She has an uncanny ability to reach into her soul and pull out something that all of us have experienced or felt sometime in our lives but are unable to put into words. She does not have any problem finding words. Chad, on the other hand, is a big ol' mess. A good mess, but a monkey-face-making mess nonetheless. But the boy sure can sing him some Ray LaMontagne's "Trouble," if I do say so myself.

I know this because Chris and I had the honor of having them stay in our home for a weekend. We'd never met them face-to-face before. We'd only talked on the phone a few times and e-mailed a little more often. But even though I'd never hugged Sarah or had a cup of coffee with her, I knew her. In a strange sort of way, I knew her. And I realized that our friendship turned out to be exactly what I expected—easy. It was like we'd known each other for years when we hugged each other for the first time at the bottom of the escalator at the Will Rogers World Airport in Oklahoma City that December afternoon.

Chad and Sarah are special to us because they aren't afraid to use the pain in their own lives to help others. You'll want to hear from this wonderful duo.

‹œ››

CINDY: Chad, what was your initial response when you found out about Sarah's infidelity?

CHAD: My initial reaction was first surprise and then shock. The shock came when she told me who it was with—a close friend of mine.

CINDY: Sarah, did you ever think you'd "do such a thing" as commit adultery?

SARAH: No. Of course not. I'm a pastor's kid who grew up at youth conferences and retreats. I never thought I'd make the kind of choices that would end me up there.

CINDY: Chad, did you ever consider getting a divorce?

CHAD: I thought about leaving for a brief moment. It was brief because of the way Sarah responded to getting caught. There wasn't a moment that she wasn't repentant and humble. Take this within context: She made it very easy to forgive and want to stay married. None of this was easy, but it was easier because of the state of her heart and attitude throughout the entire process.

CINDY: Chad, how have you been able to forgive Sarah?

CHAD: It was instant with lots of follow-up! Since forgiving her on that day, I have never once even thought to bring it up and use what she did as a weapon in our disagreements. Not once has she been defensive, and she has willingly answered any question I've asked. She takes full responsibility for the pain and hurt she caused.

CINDY: Sarah, do you ever find yourself walking in shame because of what you did? What does living in brokenness mean for you?

SARAH: Absolutely. When I get a nasty comment or a bad e-mail from a blog reader, or when I suddenly feel the weight of my own humanity, I do walk in shame. It happens more often than I'd like it to. Once in a while, the heaviness of sin is bigger than the heaviness of grace, and I feel shamed for the things I've done. I think constant brokenness is essential for living in freedom from sin. For me, it's a continual recognition that I haven't arrived, that God will always teach me something if I let Him, and that I have to be diligent to keep my heart soft and pliable. I think that's living in brokenness.

CINDY: What about trust?

CHAD: She made it easy to trust her. She made it a point to expose everything and leave nothing to chance or suspicion. She openly shares account passwords, she leaves her phone lying around and her laptop running on the kitchen table, and so on. Nothing is off-limits to me.

SARAH: In the first few weeks of recovery, I stayed with people all the time. I wanted to be above reproach in everything. When I decided to do the unthinkable, I signed up for lifelong consequences. Very quickly Chad and I set up new boundaries for our interactions with the opposite sex, and we stuck to them. In addition to the boundaries and complete honesty, we have allowed each other the power of vetoing anything we don't feel comfortable or right about. No explanation needed. It might just be a gut feeling. We've only had to use that once in a while, but I think it's important to know that our spouse will help to protect us from things we can't see ourselves and that neither of us will go forward with something that the other doesn't deem wise in this area.

It think it took a while for my husband to regain trust again. And in reality, none of us can be sure, beyond a shadow of a doubt, that someone we love will never hurt us again. He can't be sure I won't do it again. But we can center our lives together around Jesus, and my husband can trust the work of the Holy Spirit in me. He doesn't trust me. He trusts Jesus in me. And that's all any of us can do.

CINDY: How is your marriage today?

CHAD: Our marriage is great, but it takes a ton of work to keep it great. We have lapses in communication, and we fall back into some of our old habits. But now we have tools that help us see when we are slipping, and we have practical steps, which we learned from a professional counselor, that we can take to get things back on track.

SARAH: We aren't perfect. There is conflict, but the difference is in the way the conflict ends and in the state of our hearts when all is said and done. He loves me. And I adore him. I'm in for the long haul. We both are. And we do the best we can to keep Christ at the center of all we do. With Him as our anchor, I know we won't be lost in a storm again.

⟨∞⟩

Precious. They are just precious. Chris and I are so proud of them for their willingness to be a voice of hope to an aching world. To read more about their story and to experience the blessing of Sarah's writings, go to her blog at www.sarahmarkley.com.

13

Better than New

I AM FRIENDS WITH THE WOMAN my husband had an affair with. We get along terrifically.

How's that for normal?

Normalcy. We want it, crave it, desire it, can't live without it. Most of us don't like the feeling of being abnormal or of having our regular pattern in life come to a screeching halt. I know that feeling well.

But what is normalcy? We have this idea that normal means events happening according to plan and things just feeling right and everything having its place and nothing contradicting the way we think things should be. Really, though, normal is ever-changing because what is normal to you might not be normal to me. And when your life completely changes, you do realize that along the path to healing you have adopted a new normal, even if it is a version of life you resisted. Even if it includes a past or a betrayal that you never thought would be a part of your story. You wake up one day and realize that amazingly, your new normal is a place where God is doing great things.

Longing for the Way Things Were

After Chris' confession to me, I would have given just about anything to get back to the way things were. My normal state of being was ripped away from me, and I was floundering around like a fish on a beach. I wanted to go back to my life as a wife, mom, worship leader, mentor, daughter, sister, and friend. I wanted all those normal relationships and a day's worth of normal activities without this new burden and brokenness, without these obstacles to overcome from the minute my feet touched the floor in the morning. I had been fairly comfortable with life when each day was similar to the day prior.

However, after some time and a whole lot of hard work, I learned to embrace my new life, my new normal. I could have remained a victim and chosen to wallow in my pity, but I decided the time had come to show what character I hoped I had developed over the years as a follower of Christ. This was truly where the rubber met the road for me.

The part of our new normal that most people find odd is that we do have an amazing, healthy relationship with Chris' son, Ben, and his mother, Michelle. I communicate with Michelle most of the time; it just seems to work out that way. I am referred to as "Momma Cindy" by my stepson and even receive Mother's Day cards.

He spends time with us at Christmas and has an extended stay during the summer. We take our family trip when he is with us. He calls my mom Nina just as my own sons do, and she answers him as if he were her very own grandchild. My friends refer to him as if I gave birth to him and treat him no differently. He's one of my boys.

Of course, he's a child, and it wasn't his fault how he entered into this world. Many people find my acts noble and even shake their heads in awe that I love him so much. I do the same thing when I think about how much my heavenly Father loves me.

Milestone of Miracles

In your new version of normal, if you pay attention, you will discover many miracles. As I mentioned at the start of this chapter, I get along well with Michelle. I like her. A lot. She's funny and witty and kind and tenderhearted. And if our friendship isn't a miracle, I don't know what is.

Not only do I care about Michelle, but she is genuinely interested in me. We talk about the joys and sorrows of motherhood. We don't spend a lot of time together, but when we do see each other, our times are often filled with laughter. I actually look forward to seeing her. I like to hear about her work and her day-to-day life. She's exactly the kind of friend I would choose.

That may sound a little over the top to you. In fact, it might even creep you out. I can understand that. I never dreamed I would feel this way about her and that we would get along as well as we do. What I can't understand, however, is why some people won't allow God to use the most horrible of circumstances to teach them life lessons they desperately need to learn. I've learned one huge, life-changing truth in this journey: God is completely able and willing to do *anything* to bring glory to His name—even have a pastor's wife befriend her husband's ex-mistress.

It's our new normal. And yes, it could be called weird.

But if weird means choosing to make the best of a situation that nearly killed you, I'm game. If weird means allowing God to do a work in you so that someone can get a glimpse of Jesus, bring it on. If weird means deciding to work together to make a little boy's life easier, I'm all over that. If weird means making an effort to get to know her better as a friend, I'll sign on for weird.

When Ben is here visiting us, we like to take lots of pictures and videos. After he leaves, we put together a DVD for Michelle and Ben to watch. They love the DVDs we send and always share them with their friends and family nearby. This is what Michelle wrote back to me after receiving one of our DVDs.

> Just wanted to say hello and thanks again for everything you do for us. Your entire family enriches our life is so many ways. I don't want you to take this in the wrong way, but I tell my friends all the time that Chris was the best mistake I

ever made. I know it brought so much pain to you, and *that* I regret. I can deal with the misery it caused me; I deserved it but you did not. With that said, I still have received far more joy than pain. If it were not for Chris, I would not have my son, nor would I know the goodness of you.

I cried like a baby when I read that. It was as if God was looking down on me with a smile so big that my heart melted into a pool of tears. At that moment, I believed with everything in me that all the pain, misery, heartache, and devastation I experienced was worth it. All because someone might have gotten a glimpse of Jesus through my meager attempts to show a Savior. And I realized how very small I was that the Creator of the universe would use my life, my actions, to touch another's soul. As Francis Chan says in his book *Crazy Love*, "The point of my life is to point to Him." It really is all about Him and nothing about me.

Never, ever underestimate the power of God in the life of someone who is fully submitted and yielded to His plan, someone who truly believes that He does have plans to prosper them and not to harm them (Jeremiah 29:11). Praying prayers of surrender used to be so frightening for me. I wasn't sure if I really wanted what God wanted for me, simply because I couldn't see it. Now, after all I've been through in my life, I look forward to praying those prayers because I know His plans are better than mine. I look forward to yielding my mediocre, run-of-the-mill ideas to see what miracles He has on the horizon.

A New Life Needs Nurturing

Our new version of life is filled with a lot of changes. Many of the conversations between Chris and me have been about what happened. I didn't bring them up as ammunition but as a way to better understand my husband and his struggle. We've communicated about everything. We had to. Our marriage and its successful restoration depended on that communication. Without it, our relationship surely would have died.

Healing from a marital tragedy takes a lot of time and effort. It takes willingness from both the husband and the wife to do whatever it takes to make the marriage work. And I do mean whatever it takes. You have to tend to your marriage and to your new version of life with every ounce of care and energy you can muster. Initially, that might be very little because you'll be weary and uncertain. But stay the course, gain strength, and walk in God's truths for healing, and you will find what it takes to nurture this new version of wholeness.

If it means forgoing seeing a movie that you've really wanted to see because there might be raunchy, inappropriate scenes in it, you do it. If it means you really want to go visit some friends or family members but your husband is uncomfortable being alone because he doesn't trust himself, you don't go. If it means you remove your computer or Internet service from your home for a while, you do it. These acts may seem extreme and unfair to the spouse who wasn't unfaithful, to the one who has stayed true to his or her covenant, but trust me, this is what sacrifice is all about. It includes giving up something you love, like movies, computers, and traveling, for something you love more—your spouse. Sacrifice always yields fruit in the life of a believer.

We've spoken to many couples over the years who can't function as a team. One of them is willing, but the other isn't. One of them is pushing through the pain and making superhuman attempts to salvage the damaged marriage, but the other is playing the blame game or just wondering why his or her wounded partner can't seem to get over it. I can say with absolute certainty that if one spouse has this mind-set, the marriage will not succeed. Sure, you may stay married, but trust me, the covenant is broken, and the future will be bleak at best.

Chris and I are not perfect, we have never said we were perfect, and we don't expect to achieve perfection in this lifetime, but we certainly have worked our tails off cleaning up the mess we were in. We have resisted the temptation to say "woe is me," we have refused to accept a level of mediocrity that wasn't ever intended for our lives, and we have agreed to push through the pain.

Looking back on some of the days and the pain associated with them stirs something so deep in me. Not a regret, but an overwhelming sense of awe that we endured one of the most devastating situations any marriage could ever go through. There were days early on when I had no idea how this would all play out. I didn't know what the future held and whether my future would include my husband.

But I knew my God. I knew my God well enough to know His voice. So when He spoke to me and asked me to trust Him, I knew I could. I've always known I could. I still trust Him today.

Share What God Is Doing

I can tell you that the best way we've healed is not only by talking openly with each other but also by telling our story. Over and over and over again. We've spent hours upon hours walking couples through the early stages of their healing right in our living room. We've offered hope to them just by telling what happened to us and how we dealt with such a blow. And the funny thing is, all we did was share. We didn't offer any magic potion, amazing strategy, or professional therapy. We just talked. And cried. Openly and in a very raw way. It was hard in the beginning, but the more we did it, the more we were comfortable with it.

Other couples may have chosen to sweep their pain under the rug and try to get back to their old normal. But we knew that our one chance for a whole, healed life together would involve radical love, trust, faith...and honesty.

Every single time Chris and I have shared our story with others, both of us have started to cry. Not an all-out sobfest, but a few tears falling down our cheeks. Those emotions represent the bittersweet joy we both feel. Bitter because we endured so much pain in our hearts, yet sweet because that pain has turned into triumph. As 2 Corinthians 4:8-9 says, we were "hard pressed on every side, but not crushed; perplexed, but not in despair; persecuted, but not abandoned; struck down, but not destroyed." The enemy of our souls did everything in his power to get our story to end in divorce. He did not succeed, praise Jesus.

Renewal Is Costly, Redemption Is Free

This kind of renewal in a broken marriage doesn't come cheap. In fact, it's quite costly. It requires sacrificing every day, crying many tears, biting one's tongue, choosing to place another's needs ahead of your own, and enduring a lot of pain.

But it is possible. Chris and I are living proof. We've traversed a major minefield over these past several years, doing our best to avoid explosions. Unfortunately, we weren't always successful. We lost parts of ourselves during the battle. But we came out on the other side as one, the way God had always intended it to be for married couples. We went through a spiritual amputation to remove the parts of each of us that got in the way of us becoming one in Christ.

The sad part is that few are willing to go to this extent. Most walk away from hurting marriages without even listening to what God is calling them to do. Throwing in the towel has become an accepted ritual in our society. Some situations in marriages warrant such an act, but most of the time, an all-out surrender to Christ and to each other can redeem the suffering you are in. If suffering isn't redeemed, why in the world did we go through it?

You may not be facing a difficult choice about your marriage or your life today, but one day you probably will. Something will come up, and you will have to decide whether you are going to fight to make it better than you ever imagined. If Chris and I can walk through the ordeal that we did, anyone can. Trust me.

As I finish this chapter, we've just spent five weeks with my stepson. He's a remarkable little boy whom we all love. The morning Chris took him back to his mom was like any other morning. Chris and our oldest son, Noah, loaded up the car with him while Seth and I gave our hugs and stayed behind. They pulled out of the driveway, and as they did, Ben's little faced popped up from the backseat, and a twinge of pain struck my heart, the kind I feel when Noah or Seth leave me when I go on a trip.

And I found myself thinking, "What is this? What is happening here? Oh, I remember now," I thought as tears streamed down my face, "I've been praying for the last few years, 'God, please let me love him like he's my own flesh and blood.'"

God certainly answers prayers. Will I be over this flood of emotions later today? Sure. It will subside, and I'll go back to my normal routine with the two little boys in my life whom I adore even when I'm frustrated with them. But for now, I'm sad.

Before you say, "Wow, Cindy, wow. That is true redemption!" please stop and say, "Wow, God. Wow! You are a Redeemer!" I appreciate your encouragement and will receive it, but I am more in awe with my heavenly Daddy than ever. In fact, I have spent time just worshipping Him because of who He is and what He does. Because just nine years ago I wished this little boy would never be in my life. I wanted my convenience and comfort back. And today? Well, today, I sit in my little study, typing on this laptop, stopping periodically to wipe the tears from my eyes because I already miss him. That is redeemed suffering.

And so we continue to walk. One foot in front of the other. Holding each other's hands and hearts as we go. Pressing in to God and allowing Him to comfort us when we need comforting. Asking Him to change us in areas where we need changing. And begging Him to free us from things that hold us in bondage.

Take the next step and join us.

It's never too late for redemption.

Your Healing Journey

1. Do you have a strong foundation in Christ? If so, what have you done to build it? If not, what do you need to do to build it?

2. Are Satan's tactics in your life obvious or subtle? Write down examples or share them with your group.

3. What guidelines do you need to set up in your marriage in order to guard against the schemes of our spiritual enemy?

4. What is something you think you'd never do? What would the circumstances have to be like for you to see yourself doing that?

5. Why do you need redemption? Ask God to shape a new normal out of the remains of your old life.

Questions and Insights with Cindy

I ASK A LOT OF QUESTIONS. If you and I ever sat down for a cup of Eight O'clock Coffee with Peppermint Mocha creamer or Sweet Italian Crème, you would learn this.

I ask questions because I love to study people. I love to learn about people. And because I've done this over the years, I've become pretty accurate at figuring out what makes people tick, smile, relax, confide, and feel heard.

I not only ask questions but also get asked lots of questions. Most of the time they come from people who read my blog. They are legitimate questions by hurting people who just need some answers from someone who has endured what they are currently enduring. And most of the time I have answers to share with them. So I tell them what I think based upon my guidebook (the Bible), the wisdom God has given me, and the things I have experienced.

Maybe you have questions right now about your situation. It doesn't necessarily have to be related to adultery. It's possible that trust has been decreased because of something else. I know of many people—some married, some single—who are walking down a road of pain right now. Some are rebuilding marriages that are broken because of lies that have been told over the years. Others are rebuilding respect that has been lost due to poor business choices and a wavering integrity. Wherever you are on your journey, I hope that maybe some of the answers that I've given to others over the years will guide you.

Help! What if I still love him?

My papers are drafted, and they are to be filed this week, but I still love him. He walked out on the kids and me, and now he wants to come back home, but I feel he simply found out the grass was not greener on the other side. I feel as if I can't hear from God because so many things are in the way—my feelings, all the horrible words said, things that were done, and so on. I feel better when he is not around, but I guess that's because I don't have to deal with reality. Lord, help me!

CINDY'S INSIGHTS

What you are feeling is completely understandable. Your husband's actions wreaked havoc in your life and in the lives of your children. The best piece of advice someone gave me might help you too: You don't have to make that decision today. If you aren't sure that getting a divorce is exactly what you want at this time, don't file the papers. It doesn't mean that you won't ever file them, because you just might. Your husband may appear remorseful and may truly be. Time will tell if he is willing to do the hard stuff it will take to have a new marriage. And in time, if his actions prove otherwise, you'll know that he didn't really have a change in heart. If you still love him and he wants to rebuild your family, I can't see what it would hurt for you to postpone filing for a divorce. I am praying that God will make it clear to you during this season of waiting. Trust Him to heal your heart and bring peace to a difficult situation.

When does it stop hurting?

My situation is so different from yours, yet there are similarities. Three weeks ago, my husband confessed to me his unfaithfulness a year earlier—after only two months of marriage. I knew something was going on. One he had sex with; three others he kissed. That doesn't include the few during our short courtship. I actually stumbled across your story during that time.

I know my husband has grown and changed. The courage of his confession is evidence of his walk with God. All I want to know right now is, when does it stop hurting?

CINDY'S INSIGHTS

My answer for you is a hard one to accept. It takes time. The old adage says that time heals all wounds, and for the most part, that is true. But the other truth to this is that you will only hurt yourself more if you try to get around your pain, ignore your pain, or expedite it in any way. You heal when you grieve, and that means you have to go through the pain. By no means does it mean you should wallow in it for the rest of your life. But you've experienced a death—the death of your marriage. When there is a death, grieving occurs. And that's what you are doing. As you push through the pain, you have to allow yourself to feel the pain. People often want it to go away, and from my experiences of losing many people, it just doesn't until you've dealt with it. All you have is today. Worrying about when you will get through the pain is borrowing trouble from tomorrow.

In the midst of all of your pain, which I know is intense, ask God one question: What do You want me to learn from this? I promise you that with a heart surrendered to Him and fully willing to bring glory to His name through your pain, you will experience His healing. God can make your marriage even better than it was before.

Am I a fool?

I am in the midst of finding out that my husband is involved with another woman, and I don't know what to do next. He was broken and honest with me (as far as I can tell), and our night ended with me praying over him as he admitted he was holding himself back and cutting himself off from a true relationship with Christ. He has begged me to stay, begged me to give him another chance. And I want to. But how do I walk through this pain? What do we do? How do I deal with the combating emotions inside me?

I told him I want to forgive him and fight for our marriage, but then I wonder if I am being a fool. Or is that a lie from the enemy who seeks to destroy us?

CINDY'S INSIGHTS

"Fool me once, shame on you. Fool me twice, shame on me." Ever heard that before? Nobody enjoys being fooled. It's embarrassing and humiliating, and it was one of the things that I was most fearful of myself. I mean, what if he did it again? And then again? Am I an idiot?

Do those thoughts sound familiar? That's why it's so important to know what God is calling you to do. I believe that you have biblical grounds to remove yourself from your marriage, but that doesn't mean you have to. That's exactly what God spoke to me. He also very clearly spoke through a godly man who said, "You are a not a fool to stay and be a part of the redemptive work in a man's life." Those words were the beginning of healing for me.

We live in a world that will tell you that you are an idiot if you don't cut bait and move on. But my thought is, if I have a repentant husband who shows me that he's willing to do whatever it takes to make it work, why not give him a chance? I mean, I'm not guaranteed that a new husband won't do the same thing, because we are all capable of doing things we never imagined.

So are you a fool? I guess it depends on whose eyes you're looking through. With a humble, broken man who has owned his sin and is showing you the depth of his sorrow, I would say you aren't a fool.

∾

What if my husband won't stop watching porn?

From the outside, we appear to have the ideal marriage. And with the exception of his pornography addiction, we do. He has been candid with me about his struggle, but he has never told me he *wants* to stop. He admits that it prevents him from being close to God, that he is ashamed, and that he hates to see it hurt me so much. I ask him if he wants to overcome it, and he answers that he's tried and failed several times. He's resigned himself to it. He's handing himself over to defeat without a fight.

I want to install accountability software on our computers, but he says yes only when we can't afford to buy it. I am certain that he doesn't *want* to change, though he'd never admit it. "Maybe someday..." he says. I don't know what to do. I don't know how to fight for my husband's freedom. I can't make him want to change enough to actually change.

CINDY'S INSIGHTS

Well, you can't make him change or even want to change. He must desire freedom for himself. First, pray that he would hate his sin. I believe that until we truly hate "the sin that so easily entangles" (Hebrews 12:1), we will never find or even desire freedom. Also pray that his hard heart will become soft again. I often pray Ezekiel 36:26 over many hard-hearted people and ask God to truly do heart surgery. Finally, you could pray that God will do whatever it takes to get his attention. This is a dangerous prayer because it very well could mean that you have to suffer even more before anything changes.

I struggle with my own addiction to overeating, so I know the battle that rages within. You lick the fight one day only to fall the next. It's incredibly discouraging.

My husband knows this battle well too, as you know. Since his confession in February 2002, he has signed his e-mails, "Free, Chris." Because he is. The catalyst to that freedom was that he felt sick about his sin—sick enough to risk everything by exposing it. And once the exposure occurred, he got help from many. But the biggest source of help came from reading *The Bondage Breaker* by Neil T. Anderson. It literally changed and even saved his life. He has been walking in freedom ever since. I highly recommend this book for your husband. Pray that he will be interested in reading it. Once he does, I believe he will finally smell freedom and then hunger for more.

∽

How do you know you can trust him again?

It's been a little over a month since I found out about my husband and his "friend." He's supposedly cut off contact with her. We pretended to be happy while we were with all our relatives over the holidays. We are scheduled to start seeing a marriage counselor, but I still feel a million miles apart from him. I don't really like him anymore and am not sure I want to be married to him.

How did you learn to trust your husband again? And what did he do to convince you he really loved you? I'm not so sure my husband really does love me or wants to be married to me even though he is going through some of the motions.

CINDY'S INSIGHTS

Your e-mail is loaded with things I could address, but since you asked about learning to trust again, I will focus on that. This question is actually the second-most frequently asked question I receive. (The first is, "How did you ever forgive him?")

I learned to trust my husband again by placing my full trust in God. You see, I knew that God called me to stay in my marriage and work it out. Because I knew that, I knew I could trust Him regardless of the future. God is the only constant in my life. People in my life will let me down and fail me. It's a given. So expecting my husband to suddenly be trustworthy after spending years causing trust to dwindle in our marriage was ridiculous.

So I trusted God instead.

And slowly, my husband made major adjustments to his life. He began to truly desire accountability, and he built it into his life to keep him free. My husband gives me access to anything in his life and withholds nothing from me. He calls me when he leaves work and lets me know when to expect him. He never stays in a hotel alone but instead stays with friends if he has to travel overnight. He actually prefers to travel with someone and usually does. He doesn't get defensive, nor does he expect me to "just get over it" because he knows that his actions caused us to be on this path in the first place.

I truly believe that you can learn to trust again. I often tell people that time will tell whether people's hearts are truly broken over their sin or they are just sad that they got caught. I am praying that your husband is broken and will do whatever it takes to earn your trust back.

∞

Do you picture him with the other woman?

I have to keep reminding myself that I can't fix this overnight, that the road to restoration will be long and painful. I keep reminding myself that I can't learn everything right now to make it all better (even though I want to). Is it something you still fight about?

CINDY'S INSIGHTS

We are nine years into our story, so we don't ever fight about it, and we haven't for years. We haven't needed to. My husband took ownership of his sin and never expected me to get over things. He knows that his actions have lifelong consequences. And I have never thrown it back in his face. We still talk about everything because it's become a big part of our ministry, but it's never in anger or frustration. We have walked through the pain together and are on the other side. It still hurts from time to time, but we push through it together.

ᏬᏬ

How do we break the emotional tie with the other person?

My wife wants to work on rebuilding our relationship, but she still has feelings for the man she had the affair with. How do we move forward when there are feelings of attachment involved?

CINDY'S INSIGHTS

I have spoken with many who want to know how to get their spouse to "fall in love" with them again. If you do more nice things or make things better at home or get the children to behave better, will her feelings change back? You and I both know feelings are often misleading. I don't doubt that she can feel something for the other man, but are those feelings based on reality?

Adulterous relationships are based on deception. There is no truth involved. My husband ministers to many people who say they are "in love" with the person they cheated with. He helps them see that their feelings are based on an illusion. Their relationship is not real; it's hidden and forbidden, which usually makes it more exciting. It's based on lust, not love.

Those who have gotten caught up in adultery have found something that seemed to be a little more exciting and passionate, so they focused their efforts there. I know from experience that where you focus your efforts, your desire will follow.

Even though my husband was with numerous women, he never let his heart get involved. Nonetheless, we had to deal with this to an extent. Michelle is in our lives, and thankfully, we've all managed to work together. And Chris has to make sure that his interaction with her doesn't wound my heart again.

Intentionality is the key to turning your heart back toward your spouse. This goes for the one who strayed and the one who stayed committed. You both have to return to your relationship with a willingness to renew it, nurture it, and rebuild it. Don't expect it to happen quickly or in a certain way. If you are both willing, this is the path of progress. Start dating each other again. Become friends. Pay attention to what the other person needs. Open up to each other. Enjoy shared activities. If you need to cut yourself off from your old world, do it. Your marriage is worth it.

∞

What do I do about the thoughts?

I am five months into this journey, and I'm wondering if our marriage is worth the struggle because I have so many thoughts, images, and questions swirling around in my mind. How did you (or how do you) deal with the struggles of a wondering and wandering mind?

⤜∞⤚

CINDY'S INSIGHTS

For a season after Chris' confession, we weren't intimate. How could we be? That was the last thing I could even think about. This lasted for weeks for us, but for some couples, it lasts for months. The images were in my head almost constantly in the early days even when we weren't intimate. But eventually I began to combat those images and replace them with the truth. I had to follow the apostle Paul's example and "take captive every thought to make it obedient to Christ" (2 Corinthians 10:5), and then I said a verse out loud that helped take my mind off those thoughts. Then I prayed and asked God to continue to renew my mind by removing those images.

Sometimes I did that 30 times a day, or so it felt. The more I did it, the less I needed to. I was performing major mental gymnastics. It's hard work, but it will help if you don't give up. Focus on getting through today, and before you know it, you'll have endured a year of todays—and you'll be stronger for it.

Where do we begin?

Today my husband confessed that he has been sleeping with prosti-tutes. I'm numb in shock and can't believe the man I've been with for a decade has been sleeping with prostitutes for most of that time. Before we were married, he confessed to sleeping with different women, but I thought we'd put that behind us. He confessed to me on my lunch break that he'd slept with a prostitute this morning.

What do I do with that? He's not an emotional man, but he was bawling like a baby. He says he wants help and even called one coun-seling center, but we can't afford their treatment. He admitted he's a porn addict. I'm sorry to ramble—I'm just lost. Please pray for us.

CINDY'S INSIGHTS

First of all, it's not about you. Do you believe that? It's the truth. I know right now you feel dirty because of what he did, and you probably feel as if you aren't enough for him or good enough for him. I've talked to more women than I can remember who have felt similar feelings. But focus on this: When you are married to an addict, it's about the addict. The addict will do whatever is necessary for the next fix. That's the saga of addiction. <u>I know you hurt, and rightly so, but your husband needs help.</u>

Whether you choose to stay with him is just that: your choice. You don't have to stay, but I encourage you to ask God what His will is. You might be the one who can provide the very help and support your husband needs. Not only that, but he could truly see grace lived out in his life by your willingness to stay. This is all assuming that he is truly broken and wants to be free from his addiction. I have seen many marriages survive this. Don't lose hope.

Notes

1. Josh McDowell, *A Ready Defense* (Nashville: Thomas Nelson, 1990), 13-33.

2. Beth Moore, *When Godly People Do Ungodly Things* (Nashville: Broadman & Holman, 2002), 7.

3. "What Is Grief?" *Caring Connections,* www.caringinfo.org/i4a/pages/index.cfm?pageid=3369.

4. *NIV Life Application Study Bible* (Grand Rapids: Zondervan, 1997), 1655.

ACKNOWLEDGMENTS

Harvest House Publishers: Thank you for making everything practically painless through this journey. And for giving me Hope Lyda, the best substantive editor known to man. (Hope, you absolutely, without a doubt rock the house!)

LaRae Weikert and Carolyn McCready: Thank you for taking a chance on this budding author. Let's eat Mexican food together again, okay?

Lisa Whittle: We are kindred spirits, you and I. You believed in our story before we even met. Thank you for connecting me to Harvest House.

Michael Hall: Fifteen years of friendship and I still can't get you off my back. Thank you for getting this whole publishing journey started. I do love you, my bald brother.

Toben Heim: You are totally brill. I appreciate the hours upon hours you spent pouring into my manuscript before any publisher came into the scene.

Steve and Barbara Uhlmann: You loved our story before you even knew us. I love your passion for restored marriages. Thank you for your amazing support.

LifeChurch.tv staff and congregation: Your unending support of Chris and me for more than nine years astounds me. Thank you for going above and beyond to love us.

Craig and Amy Groeschel: You are like *Star Trek*—you dared to boldly go where no man has gone before. Most people wouldn't have stood by us the way you did. My gratitude runs deep for you both, and so does my love.

Jim and Beth Kuykendall: What can I even say? I've thanked you a million times, I'm sure. Thanks for the late nights and for including us as your own family. We are forever and ever grateful.

The couples who allowed me to share their stories: God is redeeming your suffering with each marriage you influence. Thank you for your willingness to share your painful journey.

BSers: (BS stands for Bible Study, people. Get your mind out of the gutter.) You believed in this book and in me way before I let myself believe. Thank you for being my inner circle and protecting my heart. Love you all so big.

My mom, Nancy: Thank you for your undying loyalty and constant support. You're my biggest cheerleader. It has not gone unnoticed.

My big brothers, Mark and David: Thank you for loving your little sister and not punching her in the arm anymore. I can always count on the two of you.

My mother-in-love, Claire Beall: Your never-ending encouragement is a powerful force in my life. They broke the mold when you were born.

My Beall siblings: I can't believe I have you all in my life. Thank you for supporting, loving, and accepting me as if I were your own sister. Wait, I'm not?

Michelle and Ben: You are two of the sweetest blessings in my life. I never imagined I'd be able to write those words. Just goes to show you how remarkable our God is. I love you both so much.

My boys, Noah and Seth: I absolutely love being your mom. Noah, thank you for seeing the big picture in all of this. Seth, I can't wait for you to understand what redemption is.

The love of my life, Chris: I knew on our first date at Chili's in Austin, Texas, that I'd marry you. We've walked through some dark valleys in our 18 years of marriage. As painful as they were, I'd still choose you.

My heavenly Daddy: Tears fill my eyes when I think of who You are to me. You comforted me in my storm even though I begged You to calm it instead. I'm thankful You didn't because now I know You better.

My readers: Regardless of whether you've endured infidelity or another type of betrayal in your marriage, I pray you are encouraged by our story. It's a story of hope and redemption. Not only that, but it's a testimony to the greatness of our God. He is so good.

ABOUT THE AUTHOR

Cindy Beall is a Christ-following writer and mentor to women. When not functioning as a domestic goddess, which includes being the wife of Chris and the mom of musical, energetic boys, Cindy enjoys ministering to others who are seeking emotional healing in their lives and marriages. Cindy loves watching Texas Longhorn sports, eating milk duds during movies, wearing jeans from The Gap, and sitting outside on the back porch with her guys.

Cindy serves as the women's ministry leader of the Oklahoma City Campus of LifeChurch.tv, where Chris is the pastor. Their hearts beat for the local church.

Healing Your Marriage When Trust Is Broken is Cindy's first published book. You can follow Cindy on Twitter (@cindybeall) and read her writings and contact her at www.cindybeall.com.

Other Great Harvest House Books You'll Enjoy

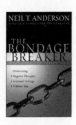

THE BONDAGE BREAKER®

Neil T. Anderson

This powerful guide has helped more than 1.3 million readers like you break away from negative thoughts and actions and experience the freedom that comes from living out your true identity as a child of God.

FORGIVE AND LOVE AGAIN

John Nieder and Thomas M. Thompson

This bestseller explores the importance of healing wounded relationships in a variety of settings: family, extended family, friendships, and workplace. Nieder and Thompson's warm and compassionate tone and life-changing insights combine to make this an invaluable guide when you are faced with the need to forgive and an excellent resource for pastors, counselors, and other emotional caregivers.

NINE CRITICAL MISTAKES MOST COUPLES MAKE

David Hawkins

Clinical psychologist Dr. David Hawkins shows that complex relational problems usually spring from nine destructive habits couples fall into, and he offers practical suggestions for changing the way you and your spouse relate to each other.